What "They" Say . . . What Will You Say?

There may be no more pressing issue before the contemporary church, especially churches living in these strange times in the United States, than to be reminded of Jesus' teaching about the poor and against the wealthy. We have so neglected his words, and substituted a comfortable pseudo-gospel better suited to worship Mammon than the Holy Trinity, that Christianity has become almost unrecognizable. The hour is late, but there is still time. Draper's timely *Christian Mission and Poverty* speaks into this moment not by using his own words but pointing us to true witnesses from antiquity through modernity. Every church, study group, discipleship class and individual should take, read and inwardly digest the essays in this important collection.

~ **D. Stephen Long, PhD,**
Cary M. Maguire University Professor of Ethics,
Southern Methodist University

Christian Ministry and Poverty: Wisdom from 2,000 Years of Church Leaders

© 2021. The Urban Ministry Institute. All Rights Reserved.

ISBN: 978-1-955424-05-9

Published jointly in 2021 by TUMI Press and Samuel Morris Publications

TUMI Press is a division of World Impact, Inc.

> TUMI Press
> The Urban Ministry Institute
> 3701 E. 13th Street, Suite 100
> Wichita, KS 67208

Equipping Leaders. Empowering Movements.

Samuel Morris Publications:

> Samuel Morris Publications
> Sacred Roots Project at Taylor University
> 236 W. Reade Avenue
> Upland, IN 46989

Samuel Morris Publications publishes texts in service to the evangelical church's life together and its ongoing pursuit of a deeper conformity to Jesus Christ (Galatians 4:19).

All Scripture quotations, unless otherwise noted, are taken from the HOLY BIBLE, NEW INTERNATIONAL VERSION®. NIV®. Copyright© 1973, 1978, 1984 by International Bible Society. Used by permission of Zondervan. All rights reserved.

Scripture quotations marked (ESV) are from The Holy Bible, English Standard Version, copyright © 2001 by Crossway Bible, a division of Good News Publishers. Used by permission. All Rights Reserved.

The cover illustration is an artistic rendition of a sculpture by Timothy P. Schmalz entitled *When I Was Hungry and Thirsty* and is inspired by Matthew 25. Mr. Schmalz's work is used by permission and may be found at www.sculpturebytps.com.

SACRED ROOTS SPIRITUAL CLASSICS

"Toward Ten Thousand Tozers"

Christian Ministry and Poverty:
Wisdom from 2,000 Years of Church Leaders

SACRED ROOTS SPIRITUAL CLASSICS 4

Rev. Dr. Andrew T. Draper

Table of Contents

Acknowledgments

I would like to thank the residents of South Central and Industry neighborhoods and the members of Urban Light Community Church for what they have taught me about living at the margins.

To my family: Aidan, you help me to see what it means to be created in the image of God. Alister, you help me to see what it means to persevere in the joy and love of Jesus. Leslie, your loyalty and truth-telling help me to know who I am in Jesus and to respect all people.

Thank you to Hank Voss for initiating this project and the series of spiritual classics to which it belongs.

GLOBAL MISSION

Foreword

When Hank Voss shared with me the vision of The Urban Ministry Institute (TUMI) to develop a reader's digest of historic Christian thought for contemporary Christian leaders who live and work in under-resourced communities, I was instantly excited. So many faithful pastors, teachers, leaders, and Christian workers learn how God spoke uniquely and definitively in Jesus and the Bible, but miss the vast sea of wisdom that lays in front of this singular horizon. They miss seeing how God's Word and Spirit has worked through faithful hearts from generation to generation to transform lives and the world in which they live. The reader you hold in your hand is a great forward stride in providing this generation with the practical wisdom of its forebears.

For the task of compiling and editing this volume on *Christian Mission and Poverty*, they chose Andrew Draper. My brother Andrew is a practitioner. He is a committed pastor living and working in a community facing the realities of economic decline. He is also a consummate academic and itinerate professor recognized nationally for his scholarly work. He daily practices thoughtfully reflecting on God's Word and the testimonies of those who faithfully applied it throughout the Great Tradition of the church. You can be assured this present collection of readings represents the thoughtful insight of a God-fearing scholar and the passionate heart of a faithful pastor.

I am happy to see this project in its completion. Andrew Draper has toured the vast histories of our rich Christian heritage and offers us snapshots of its glories. He lifts many great and well-known voices such as Clement of Alexandria, Catherine of Siena, and Martin Luther. But what I really appreciate is that he adds to this classical chorus the more modern notes of the incomparable Howard Thurman—who mentored Martin Luther King, Jr.—and the unconquerable Maria Skobtsova of Paris— trailblazing heroine of the academy, politics, and religion who died in a Nazi concentration camp for sheltering the lives of countless Jewish refugees in France.

Now, a word about the subject. Across the globe, God is moving in mighty and miraculous ways in poor communities. Today's prognosticators and statisticians announce the decline of the church in the West, but God is fomenting a powerful revival from among the disinherited. And this is not a new thing. God has done this many times over the generations. If we are to understand properly this move of God today, we should look at how the God of the Bible has historically worked in the church. I commend this edition as an excellent entrée into this great heritage of ours.

Rev. Dr. Kwesi Kamau
Lead Pastor of IMPACT Church, Dallas

Introduction

Christianity is the faith of the poor. As Christians, we worship the Lord Jesus Christ, who "though he was rich, yet for your sake became poor, so that by his poverty you might become rich" (2 Cor 8:9). This same Jesus taught his followers that the kingdom of heaven belongs to "you who are poor" and "the poor in spirit" (Luke 6:20; Matt 5:3). He also proclaimed that judgment before his throne will hinge on how his followers treated those who were hungry, thirsty, strangers, unclothed, sick, and in prison— the ones he calls "the least of these my brothers" (Matt 25:31–46).

When my wife and I joined several other families in moving into the South Central neighborhood of Muncie, Indiana in February of 2004, we did so with a desire to engage in Christian mission among those affected by poverty.[1] Like many midwestern towns, Muncie has been

---

1   Muncie is one of the poorest cities of its size in the United States, with almost a third of its residents living below the federal poverty line and only half of the homes owner-occupied (https://www.census.gov/quickfacts/munciecityindiana).

subject to job loss and economic decline. When jobs
leave, many other social problems spring up, initiating
vicious cycles that marginalize people. The tax base is
affected, which affects educational options, which affects
future employment opportunities, and so on. The housing
market is affected, which dampens new investment, which
discourages new business startup, which affects future
income potential, and so on. Illegal methods of getting
money spring up and laws are passed which target those
in poverty, which increases policing in poor neighborhoods,
which leads to a disproportionate increase in arrests, which
increases jail populations, which encourages recidivism
upon supervised release, which sustains mass incarceration,
and so on. Addiction becomes a major public health crisis
but treatment is often underfunded. Violence is instigated
as people fight from boredom and for position and resources;
military recruiters enlist young people affected by poverty;
police with military combat gear descend on the community
fighting a War on Drugs.

In the sixteen years I have lived in Muncie, the closing of
two factories took eleven thousand jobs. The two largest
employers in our town are now a university and a hospital.
This means that blue collar workers who had earned a
living wage are now required to get a new education in
order to qualify for entry-level positions. While the city
has been working hard to attract new companies, it is an
uphill battle. Additionally, much of the city's community
development resources must be used to tear down blighted
houses. Meanwhile, many people with resources move to
the suburbs or surrounding rural communities, transfer
their children out of schools in the city, or leave altogether
to pursue promising careers elsewhere. As Christians

engage in these patterns, churches leave and once vibrant faith communities decline.

In the early days of living in Muncie, many fellow Christians from other communities praised us for ministering in neighborhoods to which many of them were reluctant to go. While our community regularly experiences the perils of violence, the realities of addiction, the struggles of underfunded education, and the pain of incarceration, it remains a wonderful place to live. Our neighbors look out for each other and pitch in to beautify our community. Our streets still have sidewalks; our houses have front porches instead of privacy-fenced patios. Our community is diverse ethnically and socioeconomically. We have public parks and gardens, and community block parties open to all. Many of our friends affected by poverty are readily willing to share what little they have with others in need. As those of us who worship together engage in holistic community development work and try to love our neighbors well, we do not think of our work as bringing dignity to people. We recognize that people already have inherent dignity because we are all created in the image of God.

In speaking about Christian mission and poverty, I hesitate to use the phrase "the poor" because it can objectify[2] people by identifying them by their poverty. It can also encourage the assumption that those who are identified as "the poor" are simply recipients of Christian mission rather than people who participate in the Christian faith in active ways. At the same time, we must acknowledge that

---

2   When I use this word, I am referring to ways of thinking that picture people as objects to be studied or "ministered to" rather than sisters and brothers to be in relationship with.

Scripture names "the poor" as central to the Gospel in important ways. By investigating what this means, we can grow in understanding how Jesus uses the phrase "the poor" and how Jesus' words overturn many common ways our society thinks about poverty.

As we listen to Jesus, we learn that many people in material poverty are rich in the things of the kingdom. I have certainly found this to be the case as people who are underemployed or who rely on public assistance are often very generous toward their church and community. Conversely, as we listen to Jesus, we hear that a person can be rich in material goods and yet poor in spiritual goods. Jesus is getting at this idea when he says that it is difficult for a rich person to enter the kingdom of heaven (Matt 19:23). Jesus proclaims the kingdom as a great role reversal in which the "first will be last and the last first" (Matt 19:30). Christ includes both rich and poor in his kingdom yet consistently emphasizes the centrality of people who are poor in his messianic mission.

This is not to idealize poverty or to pretend that not having one's daily needs met is a good thing. Poverty is not a romantic state of being but is often a crushing reality under which people are consigned to suffer. The lack of stability my neighbors experience and the mold-infested houses in which many live are not to be desired. Lacking a working furnace in the winter, heating one's home with an open oven, or a child scraping together what little food is left in the cupboards are all tragedies.

Meanwhile, Christians often argue about whether poverty is the result of a failure of personal responsibility or a failure of systems stacked against people in poverty. The

Scriptures offer various perspectives on this question. In the Bible, poverty is sometimes presented as the result of a lack of initiative on the part of individuals (see Prov 6:10–11). However, more often, the text presents poverty as the result of oppression from people who are rich and systems that support unjust accumulation of wealth (see Isaiah 5, Amos 4, and Micah 3, for instance).

Either way, the Bible does not focus as much on the causes of poverty as on what the people of God are to do about it. God's people are to "seek justice, correct oppression, bring justice to the fatherless, plead the widow's cause" (Isa 1:17). They are to put away the "melody of [their] harps" and instead "let justice roll down like waters" (Amos 5:24). They are to "do justice, love mercy, and walk humbly with [their] God" (Mic 6:8). The early Jewish Christians sold land and shared resources so that "there was not a needy person among them" (Acts 4:34) and even developed systems to provide food to those most in need (Acts 6:1–7; 1 Tim 5:3–16). The people of God are the community in which the poor are central and are not pushed to the side. Today, church communities engage in this work in a variety of ways.

Both charity and justice for people who are poor have always been part of the Christian tradition. Charity entails giving or providing resources to people in need; justice means correcting or resisting systems that make people poor in the first place. Some Christians tend to favor charity programs that provide things like food, clothing, or temporary housing to individuals or families in need. Some Christians seek to correct injustice by fighting against structural forces like predatory lending or human trafficking. Still other Christians work toward development at the level of root causes of poverty by addressing needs related to employment, education or health care.

After several years of living and ministering in our under-resourced community, I became aware that I could no longer talk about our neighborhood and neighbors in a way that I would be ashamed to do were we together. I was no longer able to share "success stories" at conferences for the benefit of outsiders in a way that objectified my friends and parishioners. I was no longer able to view my work as Christian mission to the poor in a way that didn't value what I was receiving as well. I began to see the paternalism[3] inherent in picturing wealthy Christians as the prime actors in Christian mission and poor Christians as the objects of Christian mission. I saw that living together across socioeconomic and ethnic lines simply means being the body of Christ together. While it's true that our community is in need of economic resources, it's also true that there are deep (and often unrecognized) ways in which wealthy Christians need to learn from their sisters and brothers living in poverty.

As we advocate for economic and social justice or provide space for our neighbors to speak about their needs for justice, we are often viewed as strange or subversive. It can be difficult to raise funds when we are unwilling to picture our neighbors primarily as recipients of charity. If we give things away, we are likely to be praised. If we work toward the redistribution of power and economic resources, we are likely to be looked upon with suspicion. I have often reflected on the words of the Brazilian Archbishop Dom Hélder Câmara: "When I give food to

---

3 Paternalism – imagining that you know better what other people need than they do, picturing yourself in the role of a parent to children.

the poor, they call me a saint. When I ask why the poor have no food, they call me a communist."[4]

How do we discern the best responses to poverty? How should we as ministers, church leaders, and businesspeople engage in our communities? What does the Christian faith have to say about poverty? Sometimes it seems that we in the modern American church stand on opposite sides of an impassible gulf as we talk about poverty and justice. Thankfully, there are mothers and fathers of the faith who have thought long and hard about poverty and what Christian mission does and says about it. They are people who, like us, had to figure out how to follow Jesus in their own times and places in regard to these crucial questions. They came to conclusions about poverty and what it means to co-labor with God in God's mission with the poor.

These mothers and fathers can help us break through our contemporary gridlock in conversations related to poverty. Today, North American Christians often get so bogged down in defending our partisan political philosophies that our words are weaponized for purposes of winning arguments. Conservatives make blanket pronouncements against "socialism" while progressives make blanket pronouncements against the "free market." Christians in both camps claim they are following God's designs for society. While it is important to have political debates and while we must advocate alongside the poor when governmental or corporate decisions affect them adversely, our arguments about political theory can sometimes stop us from taking concrete and effective action in our

---

4   Dom Helder Camara and Francis McDonagh, eds. *Dom Helder Camara: Essential Writings* (Maryknoll: Orbis, 2009), 11.

communities. When this happens, we ignore the most important point in the conversation: we must first deeply know and carefully listen to our neighbors and friends who are poor. Otherwise, we can talk about "the poor" without joining our lives with people who are marginalized. As Christ identified himself with us, we must identify ourselves with one another across socioeconomic lines.

As I have listened to the mothers and fathers of the faith talk about Christian mission and poverty, I have been encouraged to resist losing heart as we navigate the complexity of ministry alongside the poor. As we listen to the mothers and fathers of the faith, we hear them focus on both individual needs and systemic justice issues. They help us move beyond our contemporary debates by reminding us that the Gospel is holistic—that it addresses spiritual, emotional, mental, physical, economic, personal, relational, and societal needs. They do not ignore the political dimensions of the Gospel but instead remind us that the Gospel makes us into a new polis—a new city, a new people, a new kingdom. This new society joins together the rich and the poor by elevating the poor into positions of importance in its new economy and calling the rich to enter without hoarding their wealth or relying on their privileged status. The marginalized are central in Jesus' kingdom. As Richard Bauckham reminds us, the movement of the Gospel is "to all by way of the least."[5]

---

5 Richard Bauckham, *Bible and Mission: Christian Witness in a Postmodern World* (Grand Rapids: Baker, 2004), 49.

Much like I am hesitant to reduce people to the designation "the poor," I also recognize that the phrase "Christian mission" has often been wedded to harmful ways of thinking, abuses of power, and colonial conquest.[6] However, followers of Jesus are still called to participate in the mission that Jesus gave to his disciples:

> Go therefore and make disciples of all nations, baptizing them in the name of the Father and of the Son and of the Holy Spirit, teaching them to observe all that I have commanded you.
>
> ~ Matthew 28:19–20

While that mission was first given to the Jewish disciples who brought the good news to those of us who are "the nations" (the *ethnos*), all followers of Jesus are commissioned to join God in God's mission in the world. What is that mission? We are to make disciples as we are going. What does it mean to be his disciples? As disciples, we follow Jesus by doing what Jesus did. We proclaim salvation from sin in Jesus' name. We proclaim the revolutionary and liberative good news of the kingdom. We proclaim that the last are first and the first are last. We proclaim a new society and a new creation in Jesus. We join Jesus in proclaiming his mission:

---

6   To read more about these claims, see Willie James Jennings, *The Christian Imagination: Theology and the Origins of Race* (New Haven: Yale University, 2010), Andrew T. Draper, *A Theology of Race and Place: Liberation and Reconciliation in the Works of Jennings and Carter* (Eugene: Pickwick, 2016), and Love L. Sechrest, Johnny Ramírez-Johnson, and Amos Yong, eds., *Can White People Be Saved? Triangulating Race, Theology, and Mission (Missiological Engagements)* (Downers Grove: IVP Academic, 2018).

> The Spirit of the Lord is upon me, because he has anointed me to proclaim good news to the poor. He has sent me to proclaim liberty to the captives and recovering of sight to the blind, to set at liberty those who are oppressed, to proclaim the year of the Lord's favor.
>
> ~ Luke 4:18–19

What are the commands of Jesus that he has commissioned us to teach? Jesus' commandments to his followers are to love God with all that we are and to love our neighbor as ourselves (Matt 22:37–39). When we love our neighbor as ourselves, we work for our neighbor to have access to the whole life we desire for ourselves, spiritually and physically. Christian mission is spiritual *and* physical. Christian mission is salvation from sin *and* liberation from oppression. Christian mission is charity *and* justice. Christian mission is personal *and* political.

When we engage in the kind of either-or thinking that encourages us to choose one or the other, we elevate adherence to an ideology above faithfulness to Jesus; we pledge allegiance to a kingdom of this world rather than God's kingdom. However, when we read the Bible with the mothers and fathers of the faith, we hear a different story—a more complete story. We hear the story of God's love for the world in redeeming the lost and setting the captive free. We hear the story of God's justice for the world in having mercy on the sinner and empowering the marginalized. We hear the story of Jesus' redemption of all creation in inaugurating God's kingdom and ushering in a new heaven and earth. We learn that Christian mission and justice for the poor cannot be separated.

How to Use This Book

This book and the series of spiritual classics to which it belongs should be read as if you're sitting down at a table over a meal or a coffee with leaders of the church from ages past. During this particular gathering, we are going to talk together about poverty. What does Basil or Clare or Martin or Catherine or Howard have to say to us about Christian mission and poverty? What they say may be surprising. It may take us a little bit to get used to how they say it, but when we listen closely we will find that they are thinking about questions similar to the ones we are asking today.

Many of us who are reading this volume, including me, are living and ministering in under-resourced contexts. We may be asking ourselves how we should think about poverty or what we should do to address human need. We may be asking how our commitment to the Lordship of Jesus Christ and our concern for social justice go together. We may be wondering how we should make money or spend money or give money away. We may not be satisfied with many of the answers we've gotten from people we've talked with or many of the values our societies have offered us. We may realize that we're lacking something in how we think about Christian mission and poverty. As we sit down with the mothers and father of the faith, they give us a huge gift. They tell us how they thought about similar issues in their times and places and give us clues about how to be faithful Christians today.

This volume assembles a diverse team of voices from throughout the Christian tradition to talk with us about Christian mission and poverty. They come from different eras in history and various places around the world. Some are women and some are men. They are diverse ethnically and culturally. They come from different church denominations and traditions: Catholic, Eastern Orthodox, Protestant, Evangelical, Charismatic, and non-Western theological traditions that do not fall neatly in these categories. They have a diversity of convictions on a host of issues, but they are all united around Jesus Christ, the Scriptures and the church. While they each have different passions and focuses, what they have to say about Christian mission and poverty forms a surprisingly united narrative. Some may focus on justice more than charity; some may favor stewardship of resources more than selling one's goods; some may be rich and some may be poor. However, all agree that to be a Christian involves thinking deeply about poverty and loving those affected by it.

I have arranged the writings in roughly chronological order[7] so that we can see how Christian thinking about poverty has developed and how later Christian writers often utilized insights from earlier generations. We begin with the *Didache*, one of the earliest Jewish Christian writings after the New Testament. It explains that the way of life involves sharing resources with the poor. Next, in *Who Is the Rich Man Who Is Being Saved?*, the Christian philosopher Clement of Alexandria maintains that

---

7　Exceptions to this rule will be noted in the introductions to a couple thinkers. At these points, there were compelling thematic reasons for me to adjust the order slightly.

following Jesus means refusing to be mastered by riches. Following this, we hear from *Benedict's Rule*, a highly influential guide for how monastic communities are to live. Benedict will stress the importance of sharing all things in common.

After this, we hear from two great church fathers of the East, Basil the Great and John Chrysostom. Each interprets a story from the Gospels to teach us how we as Christians are to live in regard to money and poverty. Basil uses the story of the rich young ruler to call wealthy Christians to the necessity of seeking justice for the poor. Chrysostom uses the story of the rich man and Lazarus to claim that a refusal to share riches with the poor is the same as stealing from them.

Next, we read the medieval abbess[8] Clare of Assisi's letter to a ruler, Agnes of Prague. In it, she praises Agnes' faithfulness to give up wealth and to wed herself to Holy Poverty. Catherine of Siena, an anchorite,[9] then talks with us about what it means to be obedient with regard to wealth. She will help us distinguish between poverty as obedience and begging as destitution. Following this reading, we hear from the medieval theologian Thomas Aquinas about theft and usury.[10]

The reformer Martin Luther then helps us understand what it means to work in light of God's provision. He uses Psalm 127 to illustrate that we are to work in obedience

---

8   Abbess – the head of an abbey of nuns.

9   Anchorite – a hermit or recluse.

10   Usury – to loan at interest, usually at unreasonably high rates or for the purchase of necessities or things that are consumed.

to God but that all we receive is due to God's provision alone. He encourages us to give up both worry and pride so we can be generous. After that, we hear from John Woolman, the Quaker abolitionist, about how poverty negatively affects people and how Christians must work to alleviate human suffering by pursuing just economic practices.

Next, the theologian Howard Thurman helps us recognize what the Gospel means for the marginalized. He shows that Christian mission is not something done for the poor, but is rather the liberative message of hope arising *from* the poor. He reintroduces us to Jesus as a poor member of a first-century oppressed ethnic and religious group. Mary of Paris, a twentieth century Orthodox nun, helps us think through what it means to be neither greedy nor stingy while living one's life in the world.

Finally, C. Rene Padilla, a Latin American evangelical, teaches us that the Gospel is holistic. With the phrase *integral mission*, he expands our view of the mission of God as meeting both spiritual and physical needs. He teaches us that evangelism, justice, and charity are all part of God's work in the world.

These readings are combined into eight chapters based on shared themes and chronology. Before each reading, I present a brief introduction of the thinker, giving background details about her or his life and work, explaining their contexts, and helping us see how they fit into the larger narrative of God's mission with the poor. Following each chapter, I ask a few questions to aid in group discussion. We recommend that you use this book and this series of books in group study. This reader is especially well-suited for study by groups who are committed to Christian ministry alongside people who are poor.

We envision cohorts of ministry leaders around the world reading or listening to these texts and then joining together to discuss the questions following each chapter. A group studying these resources does not need to feel pressure to answer all the questions. The questions are open-ended in order to get discussion started and to help your group understand what the authors are saying. They are designed to help you discern how the Lord is leading you to greater faithfulness and obedience in using money and ministering alongside the poor. We pray that we will become more faithful Christians as we listen to the mothers and fathers of the faith. These spiritual parents will help us see that Christianity is the faith of the poor.

A Prayer for Our Reading

After reflecting on God's provision for the poor and his "immeasurable providence," Catherine of Siena proclaimed that she was "as if drunk with love of true holy poverty" and prayed these words:

> O eternal Father! O fiery abyss of charity! O eternal beauty, O eternal wisdom, O eternal goodness, O eternal mercy! O hope and refuge of sinners! O immeasurable generosity! O eternal, infinite Good! O mad lover! And you have need of your creature? It seems to me, for you act as if you could not live without her, in spite of the fact that you are Life itself, and everything has life from you and nothing can have life without you. Why then are you so mad? Because

you have fallen in love with what you have made! You are pleased and delighted over her within yourself, as if you were drunk [with desire] for her salvation. She runs away from you and you go looking for her. She strays and you draw closer to her. You clothed yourself in our humanity, and nearer than that you could not have come.

And what shall I say? I will stutter, "A-a," because there is nothing else I know how to say . . .[11]

Amen.

---

11 Suzanne Noffke, *Catherine of Siena: The Dialogue*, 325.

The Text

GLOBAL MISSION

Chapter 1

Early Christian Teaching

Let your alms sweat in your hands, until you know to whom you should give.

~ The *Didache*

Say, "Certainly Christ does not prevent me from having property"... But do you see yourself overcome and overthrown by it? Leave it, throw it away, hate, renounce, flee.

~ Clement of Alexandria

THE *DIDACHE* (50–150)

Background

The word *Didache* means *teaching*. The *Didache* is one of the earliest Christian writings, written soon after the later books of the New Testament. It is subtitled *The Lord's*

Teaching Through the Twelve Apostles to the Nations. It is distinctively Jewish in tone, presenting the path of following Jesus as "the way of life" and contrasting it with "the way of death" (echoing Moses' words in Deuteronomy 30). It claims apostolic authority and is a good representation of Jewish Christian teaching. It is addressed to "the nations" (the *ethnos*), which shows that it is intended for a Gentile audience.

The *Didache* belongs to a group of early Christian writings that have been called *the apostolic fathers*. These writings are from the first generation of the church after the apostles died. This means they are important works but are not canonical (not included in the sixty-six books of the Old and New Testaments). Although the *Didache* would not be included in the Bible, several church fathers thought of it very highly alongside the New Testament.

The *Didache* has four sections: Christian ethics (how to live), the sacraments (baptism and communion), church order (organization and leadership), and the Lord's return. We will be drawing from the first section (way of life vs. way of death), which includes instruction on giving and supporting the poor.

Text

The Lord's Teaching Through the Twelve Apostles to the Nations

1. The Two Ways; The First Commandment

There are two ways, one of life and one of death; but a great difference between the two ways. The way of life, then, is this: First, you shall love God who made you; second, your neighbor as yourself; and all things whatever you don't want to occur to you, do not also do to another. And of these sayings the teaching is this: Bless those who curse you, and pray for your enemies, and fast for those who persecute you. For what reward is there, if you love those who love you? Do not also the Gentiles do the same? But love those who hate you, and you shall not have an enemy. Abstain from fleshly and worldly lusts. If someone gives you a blow upon your right cheek, turn to him the other also, and you shall be perfect. If someone presses you to go one mile, go with him two. If someone takes away your cloak, give him also your coat. If someone takes from you what is yours, do not ask for it back, for indeed you are not able. Give to everyone that asks you, and do not ask for it back; for the Father wills that to all should be given of our own blessings (free gifts). Happy is he that gives according to the commandment; for he is guiltless. Woe to him that receives; for if one in need receives, he is guiltless; but he that receives and is not in need, shall pay the penalty, why he received and for what [reason], and, coming into straits (confinement), he shall be examined concerning the things which he has done, and he shall not escape from there until he pay back the last farthing[1] (Matt 5:26). But also now concerning this, it has been said, Let your alms sweat in your hands, until you know to whom you should give.

2. *Various Precepts*

My child, him that speaks to you the word of God remember night and day; and you shall honor him as the Lord; for in the place from where lordly rule is uttered, there is the Lord. And you shall seek out day

---

1   Farthing – a unit of money smaller than a penny

by day the faces of the saints, in order that you may rest upon their words. You shall not long for division, but shall bring those who contend to peace. You shall judge righteously, you shall not favor persons when reproving for transgressions. You shall not be undecided whether it shall be or no. Do not be a stretcher forth of the hands to receive and a drawer of them back to give. If you have anything, through your hands you shall give ransom for your sins. You shall not hesitate to give, nor murmur when you give; for you shall know who is the good repayer of the hire. You shall not turn away from him that is in want, but you shall share all things with your brother, and shall not say that they are your own; for if you are partakers in that which is immortal, how much more in things which are mortal? You shall not remove your hand from your son or from your daughter, but from their youth shall teach them the fear of God (Eph 6:4). You shall not instruct anything in your bitterness upon your bondman or maidservant, who hope in the same God, lest they should ever not fear God who is over both (Eph 6:9; Col 4:1); for he comes not to call according to the outward appearance, but unto them whom the Spirit has prepared. And you bondmen shall be subject to your masters as to a type of God, in modesty and fear (Eph 6:5; Col 3:22). You shall hate all hypocrisy and everything which is not pleasing to the Lord. Do not forsake in any way the commandments of the Lord; but you shall keep what you have received, neither adding to them nor taking away from them (Deut 12:32). In the church you shall acknowledge your transgressions, and you shall not come near for your prayer with an evil conscience. This is the way of life.

CLEMENT OF ALEXANDRIA (150–215)

Background

Clement of Alexandria was a convert to Christianity who had been educated in Hellenistic (classical Greek) philosophy. He was a theologian and teacher who lived and ministered in ancient Alexandria in northern Egypt on the Mediterranean Sea. He was part of what would become known as the Alexandrian School, a collection of Christian theologians and teachers who trained many early church leaders. Alexandrian biblical interpretation tended to favor allegory rather than the more literal readings common in the school of Antioch in what is now Turkey.

During the time of Clement of Alexandria, the early church was thinking through what it meant to follow Jesus as Gentiles in the Roman Empire. How did worshipping the Lord position believers in relation to the religious and ethnic history of Judaism? How did being a disciple of Christ position people in relation to secular philosophy and the state? Clement of Alexandria would answer that latter question by trying to demonstrate how one could be a follower of Jesus and a participant in Hellenistic culture. In contrast to the Jewish tone of the *Didache*, Clement's writing shows that the Christian faith was shifting away from a Jewish cultural perspective. Thinkers such as Clement began to picture Christianity as a distinct religion, one that (given certain theological constraints) could be accommodated to various cultural practices. In this reading, Clement is interested in asking what it means for Christians to give up material goods in following Jesus while still

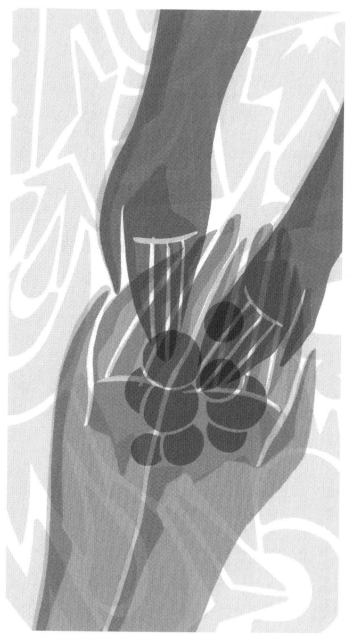

"Let your alms sweat in your hands, until you know to whom you should give."

participating in the economic systems of contemporary society. He begins what will become the common practice of offering a theological interpretation of a biblical text. His choice of the story of the "rich young ruler" will be echoed by many others.

Text

Who is the Rich Man That Shall Be Saved?

1. Those who give addresses of praise to the rich appear to me to be rightly judged not only flatterers and base, but also godless and treacherous; godless, because in neglecting to praise and glorify God, who is alone perfect and good, "from whom are all things, and by whom are all things, and for whom are all things" (Rom 11:36), they invest with divine honors men wallowing in an unpleasant and terrible life, and . . . liable on this account to the judgment of God; and treacherous, because, although wealth is of itself sufficient to puff up and corrupt the souls of its possessors, and to turn them from the path by which salvation is to be attained, they stupefy them still more, by inflating the minds of the rich with the pleasures of extravagant praises . . . and adding conceit to wealth, a heavier burden to what is already heavy by nature, from which something ought instead to be removed and taken away as being a dangerous and deadly disease . . . For it appears to me to be far kinder, than basely to flatter the rich and praise them for what is bad, to aid them in working out their salvation in every possible way . . .

2. Perhaps the reason that salvation appears more difficult to the rich than to poor men, is not a single one but is many. For some, merely hearing, and that in an off-hand way, the words of the Savior, "that it is easier for a camel to go

through the eye of a needle than for a rich man to enter into the kingdom of heaven" (Matt 19:24), despair of themselves as not destined to live, surrender all to the world, cling to the present life as if it was all that was left to them, and so diverge more from the way to the life to come, no longer asking either whom the Lord and Master calls rich, or how what is impossible to man becomes possible to God. But others rightly and adequately comprehend this, but attaching little importance to the works which tend to salvation, do not make the necessary preparations for attaining to the objects of their hope. And I affirm both of these things of the rich who have learned both the Savior's power and His glorious salvation. I have little concern for those who are ignorant of the truth.

3. Those then who are moved by a love of the truth and love of their brothers, and neither are rudely insolent towards such rich as are called, nor, on the other hand, cringe to them for their own greedy ends, must first by the word relieve them of their groundless despair, and show with the necessary explanation of the word of the Lord that the inheritance of the kingdom of heaven is not quite cut off from them if they obey the commandments; and then, in addition, exhibit and teach how and by what deeds and dispositions they shall win the objects of hope, inasmuch as it is neither out of their reach, nor, on the other hand, attained without effort . . . (as is the case with athletes) . . . So also let not the man that has been invested with worldly wealth proclaim himself excluded at the beginning from the Savior's lists . . . nor let him, on the other hand, expect to grasp the crowns of immortality without struggle and effort, continuing untrained, and without contest. But let him go and put himself under

the Word as his trainer, and Christ the President of the contest; and for his prescribed food and drink let him have the New Testament of the Lord; and for exercises, the commandments; and for elegance and ornament, the fair dispositions, love, faith, hope, knowledge of the truth, gentleness, meekness, pity, gravity: so that, when by the last trumpet the signal shall be given for the race and departure from here, as from the stadium of life, he may with a good conscience present himself victorious before the Judge who grants the rewards, confessedly worthy of the Fatherland on high, to which he returns with crowns and the praises of angels.

4. May the Savior then grant to us that . . . we may contribute to the brothers what is true, and suitable, and saving . . . He indeed grants to those who beg, and teaches those who ask, and dissolves ignorance and dispels despair, by introducing again the same words about the rich, which become their own interpreters and infallible expounders. For there is nothing like listening again to the very same statements, which till now in the Gospels were distressing you, hearing them as you did without examination . . .

> And going forth into the way, one approached and kneeled, saying, Good Master, what good thing shall I do that I may inherit everlasting life? And Jesus says, Why do you call Me good? There is none good but one, *that is*, God. You know the commandments. Do not commit adultery, Do not kill, Do not steal, Do not bear false witness, Do not defraud, Honor your father and your mother. And he answering says to Him, All these have I observed. And Jesus, looking upon him, loved him, and said, One thing you lack. If you would be perfect, sell what you have and give to the poor, and you shall have treasure in heaven: and come, follow Me.

And he was sad at that saying, and went away grieved: for he was rich, having great possessions. And Jesus looked round about, and says to His disciples, How hardly shall they that have riches enter into the kingdom of God! And the disciples were astonished at His words. But Jesus answers again, and says unto them, Children, how hard is it for them that trust in riches to enter into the kingdom of God! More easily shall a camel enter through the eye of a needle than a rich man into the kingdom of God. And they were astonished out of measure, and said, Who then can be saved? And He, looking upon them, said, What is impossible with men is possible with God. For with God all things are possible. Peter began to say to Him, Look, we have left all and followed You. And Jesus answered and said, Truly I say unto you, Whoever shall leave what is his own, parents, and brethren, and possessions, for My sake and the Gospel's, shall receive an hundred-fold now in this world, lands, and possessions, and house, and brothers, with persecutions; and in the world to come is life everlasting. But many that are first shall be last, and the last first . . .

8. . . . But, nevertheless, this man being such, is perfectly persuaded that he doesn't need anything in relation to righteousness, but that he is entirely destitute of life. This is why he asks it from Him who alone is able to give it. And with reference to the law, he carries confidence; but the Son of God he addresses in supplication . . .

9. Jesus, accordingly, does not charge him with not having fulfilled all things out of the law, but loves him, and fondly welcomes his obedience in what he had learned; but says that he is not perfect in relation to eternal life . . . For "the commandment is holy" (Rom 7:12) as far as a sort of training with fear and preparatory discipline goes . . . But Christ is the fulfilment "of the law for righteousness to

everyone that believes" (Gal 3:24); and not as a slave making slaves, but sons, and brethren, and fellow-heirs, who perform the Father's will.

10. "If you will be perfect" (Matt 19:21). Consequently he was not yet perfect . . . For choice was the man's, who was free; but the gift was God's, who is the Lord. And He gives to those who are willing and are very sincere, and ask, that so their salvation may become their own. For God does not force (for compulsion is repugnant to God), but supplies to those who seek, and give to those who ask, and opens to those who knock. If you will, then, if you really will, and are not deceiving yourself, gain what you lack. One thing is lacking you—the one thing which remains, the good, which is now above the law . . .

The one who had fulfilled all the demands of the law from his youth, and had gloried in what was magnificent, was not able to complete the whole with this one thing which was specially required by the Savior, so as to receive the eternal life which he desired. But he departed displeased, distressed by the commandment of life, which is what he had asked for. For he did not truly wish life, as he stated, but aimed at the mere reputation of the good choice. And he was capable of busying himself about many things; but the one thing, the work of life, he was powerless, and unwilling, and unable to accomplish. The Lord said a similar thing to Martha, who was occupied with many things, and distracted and troubled with serving; while she blamed her sister, because, she left her serving and set herself at His feet, devoting her time to learning: "You are troubled about many things, but Mary has chosen the good part, which shall not be taken away from her" (Luke 10:41–42). So also He called him to leave his busy life, and hold on to One and stick fast to the grace of Him who offered everlasting life.

11. What then was it that persuaded him to flee, and made him depart from the Master, from the request, the hope, the life, previously pursued with passion?—"Sell your possessions." And what is this? He does not, as some flippantly think, call him to throw away the things possessed, and abandon his property; but calls him to banish from his soul his beliefs about wealth, his excitement and unhealthy feeling about it, the anxieties, which are the thorns of existence, which choke the seed of life. For it is no great thing or desirable to be without the necessities of wealth, unless there's a special reason—unless on account of life. For therefore those who have nothing at all, but are destitute, and beggars for their daily bread, the poor dispersed on the streets, who know not God and God's righteousness, simply on account of their extreme want and destitution of subsistence, and lack even of the smallest things, were most blessed and most dear to God, and sole possessors of everlasting life . . .

12. Why then command as new, as divine, as alone life-giving, what did not save those of former days? And what peculiar thing is it that the new creature the Son of God implies and teaches? It is not the outward act which others have done, but something else indicated by it, greater, more godlike, more perfect, the stripping off of the passions from the soul itself . . . For those who formerly despised external things gave up and squandered their property, but the passions of the soul, I believe, they intensified. For they indulged in arrogance, pretension, and vain pride, and in hatred of the rest of mankind, as

if they had done something superhuman . . . One, after ridding himself of the burden of wealth, may still have the lust and desire for money inside him and alive; and may have abandoned the use of it, but being at once destitute of and desiring what he spent, may grieve even more both on account of the absence of what he had, and the presence of regret. For it is impossible and inconceivable that those who need the necessities of life shouldn't be harassed in mind, and hindered from better things in the quest to provide them somehow, and some way.

13. And how much more beneficial is the opposite for a man, who has an ability, both not to be in a tight place himself about money, and also to give assistance to those to whom it is required to give! For if no one had anything, what room would be left among men for giving? And how can this dogma fail to be found plainly opposed to and conflicting with many other excellent teachings of the Lord?

> Make to yourselves friends of the mammon[2] of unrighteousness, that when you fail, they may receive you into the everlasting dwellings (Luke 16:9). Acquire treasures in heaven, where neither moth nor rust destroys, nor thieves break through (Matt 6:19).

How could one give food to the hungry, and drink to the thirsty, clothe the naked, and shelter the homeless, for which if we don't do He threatens us with fire and the outer darkness, if each man first got rid of all these things? No, He calls Zacchaeus and Matthew, the rich tax-gathers, to entertain Him with hospitality. And He does not call them to part with their property, but,

---

2   Mammon – wealth or money

applying the just and removing the unjust judgment, He adds, "Today salvation has come to this house, because he also is a son of Abraham." He so praises the use of property as to add, along with giving a share of it, to give drink to the thirsty, bread to the hungry, to take the houseless in, and clothe the naked . . .

14. Riches, then, which also benefit our neighbors, are not to be thrown away. For they are possessions, inasmuch as they are possessed, and goods, inasmuch as they are useful and provided by God for the use of men; and they lie to our hand, and are put under our power, as material and instruments which are for good use to those who know the instrument. If you use it skillfully, it is skillful; if you are deficient in skill, it is affected by your lack of skill, being itself free of blame. Wealth is such an instrument. Are you able to make a right use of it? It is subservient to righteousness. Does one make a wrong use of it? It is, on the other hand, a minister of wrong. For its nature is to be subservient, not to rule . . .

15. . . . We must therefore renounce those possessions that cause injury, not those that are capable of giving service, if one knows how to use them rightly. And what we manage with wisdom, and sobriety, and holiness, is profitable; and what is hurtful must be cast away . . . So then the Lord introduces the use of external things, calling us to put away not the things by which we live, but the bad ways we use them . . .

16. . . . And that (soul) which is rich in lusts is unclean, and struggles with many worldly affections. For he who holds possessions, and gold, and silver, and houses, as the gifts of God; and ministers from them to the God who

gives them for the salvation of men; and knows that he possesses them more for his brothers' sake than his own; and is superior to the possession of them, and is not the slave of the things he possesses; and does not carry them about in his soul, and does not tie up and restrict his life within them, but is ever working at some good and divine work, even should he for some time or other be deprived of them, is able with cheerful mind to deal with their removal as well as he deals with their abundance. This is he who is blessed by the Lord, and called poor in spirit, a worthy heir of the kingdom of heaven, not one who could not live rich.

17. But he who carries his riches in his soul, and instead of God's Spirit bears gold or land in his heart, and is always acquiring possessions without end, and is always on the outlook for more, bending downwards and chained in the toils of the world, being earth and destined to depart to earth—how can he be able to desire and to think about the kingdom of heaven . . . ? For where the mind of man is, there is also his treasure.

. . . In the same way spiritual poverty is blessed. This is why Matthew also added, "Blessed are the poor" (Matt 5:3). How? "In spirit." And again, "Blessed are they that hunger and thirst after the righteousness of God" (Matt 5:6). This is why the opposite kind of poor are wretched, those who have no part in God, and still less in human property, and have not tasted of the righteousness of God . . .

24. You may even go against wealth. Say, "Certainly Christ does not prevent me from having property. The Lord does not envy." But do you see yourself overcome and overthrown by it? Leave it, throw it away, hate,

renounce, flee. "Even if your right eye offends you, cut it out" quickly (Matt 5:9). Better is the kingdom of God to a man with one eye, than the fire to one who is not mutilated. Whether hand, or foot, or soul, hate it. For if it is destroyed here for Christ's sake, it will be restored to life up there . . .

41. This is why it is by all means necessary for you, who are prideful, and powerful, and rich, to set over yourself some man of God as a trainer and governor. Respect him, even if it's only one man; fear him, even if it's only one man. Give yourself to hearing, even though it's only one speaking freely, using harshness, and at the same time healing. For it is good for the eyes not to be always playful, but to weep and smart sometimes, for greater health. Also, nothing is more dangerous to the soul than uninterrupted pleasure. For it is blinded by melting away, if it's not moved by bold speech. Fear this man when he's angry; be pained at his groaning; and respect him when he stops being angry; and anticipate him when he is disapproving and punishing. Let him pass many sleepless nights for you, interceding for you with God . . . For He does not hold out against His children when they beg His pity. And for you he will pray purely, held in high honor as an angel of God, and grieved not by you, but for you. This is sincere repentance. "God is not mocked" (Gal 6:7), nor does He pay attention to vain words. For He alone searches the marrow and reins of the heart, and hears those that are in the fire, and listens to those who call out to Him in the whale's belly; and is near to all who believe, and far from the ungodly if they do not repent . . .

Discussion Questions

The Didache has some things to say about discerning human need. What are the needs in your community? How can you figure out what those needs are and help meet them?

Are there any differences in the ways *The Didache* and Clement talk about giving? Which text pictures selling one's goods and giving to the poor more literally and which pictures it more figuratively? Do you agree with one more than the other?

Clement talks about the passions and desires of the soul being cast off. Are there passions or desires in you that God may want to remove, change, or redirect?

What does *The Didache* mean when it tells us not to let our alms "sweat in our hands" and not to "stretch forth" our hands to receive? What is God calling you and your community to do with your hands?

People in North America are some of the wealthiest in the world. What habit does Clement claim wealthy people must practice? What practices might God be calling North American Christians to engage in?

GLOBAL MISSION

Chapter 2

A Monastic Response

Let all things be common to all, as it is written. And do not let anyone call or take to himself anything as his own (cf. Acts 4:32). But if anyone should be found to indulge this most destructive vice, and, having been warned once and again, does not change, let him be subjected to punishment.

~ Benedict of Nursia

BENEDICT'S RULE (516)

Background

By the fifth and sixth centuries, the situation of the Christian church had changed dramatically. The faith had gone from being seen as a sect of Judaism, to being persecuted as idolatry under the Roman Empire, to being accepted into mainstream cultural trends, to becoming the favored religion of Rome under the emperor Constantine, who ruled from AD 306–337. Christians went from being relatively fringe members of society to being in seats of political and ecclesial[1] power. However, alongside the mainstreaming of the church grew an alliance with systems of worldly power and wealth. The sort of economic compromise proposed by Clement of Alexandria was considered problematic by many Christians. They believed it was necessary to pull back from alignment with political and economic power. Some of these Christians went to the "desert" (either literally or metaphorically) and formed counter-culture communities that they believed would protect crucial aspects of the faith. These monastic communities worked together, studied together, ate together, and ministered together.

These new monastic communities often needed direction as they formed new societies within the larger society. They began to develop *rules*, documents that outlined the core commitments and practices of members of the community. The most famous and influential of these rules is the *Rule of St. Benedict of Nursia*, who lived from around AD 480–547.[2] This rule is still practiced today by monastic communities known as Benedictines. It has guided the design of various rules for other monastic orders down through the ages. In general, monastic orders were formed based on the guiding vision and gifts (*charisma*) of visionary leaders. Local monastic communities were often birthed out of a monastic order and were

---

1   Ecclesial – church

2   See Benedict of Nursia and Basil of Caesarea, *Becoming a Community of Disciples: Guidelines from Abbot Benedict and Bishop Basil*, edited by Greg Peters, Sacred Roots Spiritual Classics 2 (Wichita, KS: The Urban Ministry Institute, 2021).

governed by an Abbot or Abbess. In general, monks and nuns took vows of poverty, celibacy, and obedience.

Sometimes monasticism has been pictured as an escape from the world. While pulling away from the temptations of society was certainly part of the guiding impulse for monasticism, monastic communities formed institutions and works that ministered to the poor and changed society. Not simply a retreat, monasticism sought to preserve something distinct about the Christian faith. Monastic communities founded hospitals, farms, schools, seminaries, businesses, publishing centers, artisan gatherings, homes for the poor, orphanages, homes for people with disabilities, and retreat centers, among many more works. Monastic communities were the homes of the scribes who copied the Scriptures and ancient Christian writings. Before modern printing presses, monasteries preserved the written word.

This section of *Benedict's Rule* focuses on the use, ownership, and stewardship of goods. It demonstrates how monastic communities practice their vow of poverty. Many ministries in under-resourced contexts today have drawn from monasticism in thinking about how they should be organized for mission among the poor.

Text

Benedict's Rule

1. Of the Tools and Goods of the Monastery

Let the Abbot appoint brothers whose life and character he can rely on, over the property of the monastery in tools, clothing, and general things, and let him assign to them, as he shall think is right, all the articles which must be

collected after use and stored away. Let the Abbot keep
a list of these articles, so that, when the brothers in turn
succeed each other in using them, he may know what
he gives and what he receives back. If anyone, however,
handles the goods of the monastery lazily or carelessly
let him be reprimanded and if he does not change let him
come under the discipline of the Rule.

2. *Whether Monks Ought to Have Anything of Their Own*

The vice of personal ownership must by all means be cut
out in the monastery by the very root, so that no one may
dare to give or receive anything without the command of
the Abbot; nor to have anything whatever as his own, neither
a book, nor a writing tablet, nor a pen, nor anything else
whatever, since monks are allowed to have neither their
bodies nor their wills in their own power . . . Let all things
be common to all, as it is written. And let no one call or
take to himself anything as his own (cf. Acts 4:32). But if
anyone should be found to indulge this most destructive
vice, and, having been warned once and again, does not
change, let him be subjected to punishment.

3. *Whether All Should Receive in Equal Measure What Is Necessary*

It is written, "Distribution was made to everyone according
as he had need" (Acts 4:35). We do not say by this that
respect should be had for persons (God forbid), but regard
for infirmities[3]. Let him who has need of less thank God
and not give way to sadness, but let him who has need of
more, humble himself for his infirmity, and not be

---

3   Infirmities – sicknesses or weaknesses

overjoyed at the indulgence shown him; and by this all the members will be at peace.

Above all, do not let the evil of murmuring[4] appear in the least word or sign for any reason whatever. If anyone be found guilty in this way, let him be placed under very severe discipline.

4. Of the Weekly Servers in the Kitchen

Let the brothers serve each other so that no one is excused from the work in the kitchen, except on account of sickness or more necessary work, because greater merit and more charity is acquired by this. Let help be given to the weak, however, that they may not do this work with sadness; but let all have help according to the size of the community and the circumstances of the place . . .

Let him who is to go out of the weekly service, do the cleaning on Saturday. Let him wash the towels with which the brothers wipe their hands and feet. Let him who goes out, as well as him who is to come in, wash the feet of all. Let him return the utensils of his department to the Cellarer[5] clean and whole. Let the Cellarer give the same to the one who comes in, so that he may know what he gives and what he receives back.

An hour before meal time let the weekly servers receive each a cup of drink and a piece of bread more than their prescribed portion, that they may serve their brothers at the time of refection without murmuring and undue strain. On solemn feast days, however, let them go without till after Mass.

---

4   Murmuring – complaining or gossiping

5   Cellarer – the monk responsible for providing food and drink.

As soon as the morning office[6] on Sunday is ended, let the weekly servers who come in and who go out, cast themselves upon their knees in the oratory[7] before all, asking their prayers . . .

5. Of the Sick Brethren

Before and above all things, the sick must be taken care of, that they be served in very truth as Christ is served; because He has said, "I was sick and you visited Me" (Matt 25:36). And "As long as you did it to one of these My least brothers, you did it to Me" (Matt 25:40). But let the sick themselves also consider that they are served for the honor of God, and do not let them grieve their brothers who serve them with unnecessary demands. These must, however, be served patiently, because from such as these a more bountiful reward is gained. Let the Abbot's greatest concern, therefore, be that they do not suffer neglect.

Let a cell be set apart for the sick brothers, and a God-fearing, diligent, and careful attendant be appointed to serve them. Let the use of the bath be offered to the sick as often as it is useful, but let it be granted more rarely to the healthy and especially the young. In this way also let the use of meat be granted to the sick and to the very weak for their recovery. But when they have been restored let them all go without meat in the usual manner.

But let the Abbot exercise the utmost care that the sick are not neglected by the Cellarer or the attendants, because whatever his disciples do wrongly falls back on him.

---

6   Morning Office – the prescribed order of prayers for the beginning of the day.

7   Oratory – the worship space of the monastic community.

6. *Of the Aged and Children*

Although human nature causes people to feel compassion for these life-periods, namely, old age and childhood, still, let the decree of the Rule make provision also for them. Let their natural weakness be always taken into account and let the strictness of the Rule not be kept with them in respect to food, but let there be a tender regard in their behalf and let them eat before regular hours.

7. *Of the Quantity of Food*

Making allowance for the infirmities of different persons, we believe that for the daily meal, both at the sixth and the ninth hour, two kinds of cooked food are sufficient at all meals; so that he who might not be able to eat of one, may make his meal of the other. Let two kinds of cooked food, therefore, be sufficient for all the brothers. And if there are fruit or fresh vegetables, a third may be added. Let a pound of bread be sufficient for the day, whether there is only one meal or both dinner and supper. If they are to eat supper, let a third of a pound be reserved by the Cellarer and given at supper.

If, however, the work has been especially hard, it is left to the discretion and power of the Abbot to add something, if he thinks it necessary, above all things protecting against every excess, that a monk not be overtaken by indigestion. For nothing is so contrary to Christians as excess, as our Lord says: "See that your hearts are not overcharged with excessive consumption" (Luke 21:34).

Let the same quantity of food, however, not be served out to young children but [give them] less than the older ones, observing measure in all things.

But let all except the very weak and the sick abstain altogether from eating the flesh of four-footed animals.

8. Of the Quantity of Drink

"Everyone has his proper gift from God, one after this manner and another after that" (1 Cor 7:7). It is with some hesitation, therefore, that we determine the measure of nourishment for others. However, making allowance for the weakness of the infirm, we think one hemina[8] of wine a day is sufficient for each one. But to whom God grants the endurance of abstinence, let them know that they will have their special reward. If the circumstances of the place, or the work, or the summer's heat should require more, let that depend on the judgment of the Superior, who must above all things see to it, that excess or drunkenness do not creep in.

Although we read that wine is not at all proper for monks, yet, because monks in our times cannot be persuaded of this, let us agree to this, at least, that we do not drink to the full, but sparingly; because "wine makes even wise men fall off" (Sirach[9] 19:2). But where the poverty of the place will not permit this much wine to be had, but much less, or none at all, let those who live there bless God and not murmur. This we charge above all things, that they live without murmuring.

---

8 Hemina – a unit of liquid measurement, totaling about ten fluid ounces

9 Sirach – a book from the Apocrypha, a collection of Christian writings from the intertestamental period (between Malachi and the Gospels). Roman Catholics include the Apocrypha in their Bibles; Protestants see the Apocrypha as helpful writings but not as canonical (not to be included in Scripture).

Discussion Questions

How is the community of a monastery different from the community in which you live? Are there ways that God is calling you and your fellow Christians to live differently in regard to money and ownership?

What does Benedict teach about private ownership of goods? Are there ways that your community of Christians could learn from monastic communities in this regard?

Benedict sees his fellow monks as brothers. This affects his desire that each brother might receive what he needs. How could seeing the people around you as siblings change your desires in relation to them?

There are times that Benedict thinks certain community members should have more and times when they should receive less. How do communities know the difference between these two times? Are there times God is calling you to hold on to goods and times God is calling you to give them away?

For Benedict, the discipline of living by a community rule helps Christians form a healthy community. Are there practices that you or your community could live by that would encourage a healthy view of money and human need?

GLOBAL MISSION

Chapter 3

Distribution and Justice

The man who loves his neighbor as himself will have acquired no more than what his neighbor has; whereas you, visibly, have acquired a lot. Where has this come from?

~ Basil the Great

Not only robbery of other men's goods, but also the not imparting our own good things to others . . . this also is robbery, and covetousness, and fraud.

~ John Chrysostom

BASIL THE GREAT (330–379)

Background

Basil of Caesarea is one of three theologians known as the Cappadocians: Basil, Gregory of Nazianzus, and Gregory of Nyssa. Basil and Gregory of Nyssa were brothers. Less recognized is their sister Macrina and the crucial role she played in encouraging them to study theology and practice poverty. Although Basil lived before Benedict, I offered *Benedict's Rule* first to show that monasticism was a different kind of response to the economics of the day than the type of response Clement proposed. Basil represents yet another way of thinking about Jesus' commands in relation to money, poverty, and Christian mission. While these various thinkers differed concerning the relation of money to the Christian faith, they all agreed that to participate in Christian mission meant being committed to ministry alongside the poor. They all agreed that having wealth was in some sense dangerous, even if some, like Clement, thought it was a necessary good in order to practice Christian hospitality and stewardship. Whereas Clement of Alexandria had focused on dispelling the inner attachment to wealth and Benedict of Nursia had stressed the importance of literally rejecting wealth for the sake of Christian community, Basil and the Cappadocians stressed directing wealth toward providing for the poor and correcting injustice.

Basil was born into a wealthy family in Caesarea of Cappadocia, which is in modern-day Turkey.[1] After a severe drought and in the face of famine, Basil preached and taught the responsibility of wealthy Christians to share their resources on behalf of the disenfranchised. He had to find a middle ground between the figurative approach of Clement and the literal approach of the monastics. He preached about themes related to

---

1   See Benedict of Nursia and Basil of Caesarea, *Becoming a Community of Disciples: Guidelines from Abbot Benedict and Bishop Basil*, edited by Greg Peters, Sacred Roots Spiritual Classics 2 (Wichita, KS: The Urban Ministry Institute, 2021).

social justice and encouraged Christians to act toward the alleviation of poverty. He also moved beyond focusing on the responsibility of individuals (charity) to preaching against the ways systems worked together to make and keep people poor (justice). Basil also shifted from focusing on the agency of the wealthy to the personalizing of those who were categorized as poor.[2] Basil founded institutions that provided housing, medical care, and job training.

In later readings, we will see a distinction made between the *commandments* given to all Christians and the *counsels* given to those committed to the "religious life" (monastics). Basil tried to avoid this dichotomy by proclaiming that the law of love as taught by Jesus is applicable to all who would follow him. He had the task of figuring out how to communicate this to his congregants. This sermon was delivered to wealthy parishioners during the time of the famine. Like Clement, he picks as his text the story of Jesus' interaction with the rich young ruler.

Text

Sermon to the Rich

> And, behold, one came and said unto him, Good Master, what good thing shall I do, that I may have eternal life? And he said unto him, Why do you call me good? there is none good but one, that is, God: but if you will enter into life, keep the commandments. He says unto him, Which? Jesus said, You shall do no murder, You shall not steal, You shall not bear false witness, Honor your father and your mother: and, You shall love your neighbor as yourself. The young man says unto him, All these things I have kept from my youth up: what do I yet lack? Jesus said unto him,

---

2   C. Paul Schroeder, *St. Basil the Great: On Social Justice* (Crestwood: St. Vladimir's Seminary Press, 2009), 23–25.

> If you will be perfect, go and sell what you have, and give
> to the poor, and you shall have treasure in heaven: and
> come and follow me. But when the young man heard that
> saying, he went away sorrowful: for he had great possessions.

~ Matthew 19:16–22

1. We heard about this young man the day before
yesterday, and, if you were listening attentively, you
should be able now to remember the things we were
examining then. First, that this is not the same person
as the lawyer we read of in Luke (Luke 10:25). For
that man was a tempter, inquiring insincerely; but this
one asks soundly, though he fails to accept the answer
with a ready obedience. For he would not have gone
away sorrowful after receiving such an answer from the
Lord if he had put forth his questions cynically in the
first place. Hence, it seemed to us that this man's behavior
was confused: partly commendable, as the passage
shows, and partly wretched and altogether hopeless.
For to know the one who is truly the Teacher, and,
disregarding the Pharisees' posturings, and the lawyers'
opinion, and the mob of scribes, to ascribe this name
to him who is the only true and good Teacher, so much
is praiseworthy. And moreover it is a worthy endeavor
to show concern over how one is to inherit eternal life:
this, too, must be accepted.

But what in fact proves that his whole intent was not to
seek what is truly good, but only to snoop about for what
would please the crowd, is this: when he had learned
from the true Teacher saving truths, he didn't write them

in his heart, nor did he put the teachings to practice, but he went off depressed, clouded by a schooling in avarice. Again, this demonstrates moral inconsistency and self-contradiction. You call him teacher, and you won't do his lessons? You acknowledge him to be good, and what he gives you, you throw away? But, surely, he who is good supplies good things; this is obvious. Although what you ask about is eternal life, you give proof of being utterly addicted to the enjoyment of this present life. What, after all, is this hard, heavy, burdensome word which the Teacher has put forward? "Sell what you have, and give to the poor." If he had laid upon you agricultural toils, or hazardous mercantile ventures, or so many other troubles which are incidental to the life of the wealthy, then you'd have had cause for sorrow, taking the order badly; but when he calls you by so easy a road, without toil or sweat, to show yourself an inheritor of eternal life, you are not glad for the ease of salvation, but you go away pained at heart and mourning, making useless for yourself all that you had labored at beforehand. For if, as you say, you've not murdered, nor committed adultery, nor stolen, nor witnessed against someone a false witness, you make such exertions unprofitable to you when you fail to add on the remainder, by which alone you might be able to enter into the kingdom of God. And if a physician had declared to you that he could fully mend you of some physical disfigurement you had by nature or disease, wouldn't you have heard him gladly? But when the great Physician of souls desires to make you whole of your deficiencies in things that matter most, you don't accept the favor, but mourn and put on a gloomy face.

"*You shall love your neighbor as yourself.*"

Now, you are obviously very far from having observed one commandment at least, and you falsely swore that you had kept it, namely, that you've loved your neighbor as yourself. For see: the Lord's commandment proves you to be utterly lacking in real love. For if what you've claimed were true, that you have kept from your youth the commandment of love, and have given to each person as much as to yourself, how has it come to you, this abundance of money? For it takes wealth to care for the needy: a little paid out for the necessity of each person you take on, and all at once everything gets parceled out, and is spent upon them. Thus, the man who loves his neighbor as himself will have acquired no more than what his neighbor has; whereas you, visibly, have acquired a lot. Where has this come from?

Or is it not clear, that it comes from making your private enjoyment more important than helping other people? Therefore, however much you exceed in wealth, so much so do you fall short in love: else long since you'd have taken care to be divorced from your money, if you had loved your neighbor. But now your money sticks to you closer than the limbs of your body, and he who would separate you from it grieves you more than someone who would cut off your vital parts. For if you had clothed the naked, if you had given your bread to the hungry, if you had opened your doors to every stranger, if you'd become a father to orphans, if you had suffered together with all the powerless, what possessions would now be causing you despondency? Why should you now be upset to put aside what's left, when you'd long since have taken care to distribute these things to the needy? . . .

2. But how do you make use of money? By dressing in expensive clothing? Won't two yards of tunic suffice you, and the covering of one coat satisfy all your need of clothes? But is it for food's sake that you have such a demand for wealth? One bread-loaf is enough to fill a belly. Why are you sad, then? What have you been deprived of? The status that comes from wealth? But if you would stop seeking earthly status, you should then find the true, resplendent kind that would conduct you into the kingdom of heaven. But what you love is simply to possess wealth, even if you derive no help from it. Now everyone knows that an obsession for useless things is mindless. Just so, what I am going to say should seem to you no greater paradox; and it is utterly, absolutely true. When wealth is dispersed, in the way the Lord advises, it naturally stays put; but when held back it is transferred to another. If you hoard it, you won't keep it; if you scatter, you won't lose. For (says the scripture), "He has dispersed, he has given to the poor; his righteousness endures forever" (Ps 112:9).

But it isn't for the sake of clothing or food that riches are a matter of such concern to so many people; but, by a certain wily artifice of the devil, countless pretexts of expenditure are proposed to the rich, so that they strive for superfluous, useless things as though they were necessary, and so that nothing measures up to their conception of what they should spend. For they divide up their wealth with a view to present and future uses; and they assign the one portion to themselves, and the other to their children. Next, they subdivide their expense account for various spending purposes. Hear now what sort of arrangements they make. Let some of our assets be accounted as liquid, others as fixed; and let liquid assets exceed the limits of necessity; let this much be on hand for household extravagance, let that much take care of showy visits to town. Let this tend to whoever goes on exotic voyages, and let that furnish the one who stays at home with an opulent lifestyle which will be envied by all. It amazes me, how they can pile on notions of superfluities . . .

3. Since, then, the wealth still overflows, it gets buried underground, stashed away in secret places. For (they say), "what's to come is uncertain, we may face unexpected needs." Therefore it is equally uncertain whether you will have any use for your buried gold; it is not uncertain, however, what shall be the penalty of inveterate inhumanity. For when you failed, with your thousand notions, wholly to expend your wealth, you then concealed it in the earth. A strange madness, that, when gold lies hidden with other metals, one ransacks the earth; but after it has seen the light of day, it disappears again beneath the ground. From this, I perceive, it happens to you that in burying your money you bury also your heart. "For where your treasure is," it is said, "there will your heart be also" (Matt 6:21).

This is why the commandments cause sorrow; because they have nothing to do with useless spending sprees, they make life unbearable for you. And it seems to me that the sickness of this young man, and of those who resemble him, is much like that of a traveler, who, longing to visit some city and having just about finished his way there, lodges at an inn outside the walls, where, upon some trifling impulse, he is averted, and so both makes his previous effort useless, and deprives himself of a view of the wonders of the city. And of such a nature are those who engage to do the other commandments, then turn around for the sake of gathering wealth. I've seen many who will fast, pray, groan, and display every kind of pious exertion, so long as it costs them nothing, but who will not so much as toss a red cent to those who are suffering. What good do they get from their remaining virtue? For the kingdom of heaven does not admit them; for, as it says, "It is easier for a camel to go through a needle's eye, than for a rich man to enter into the kingdom of God" (Luke 18:25).

But, while this statement is so plain, and its speaker so unerring, scarcely anyone is persuaded by it. "So how are we supposed to live without possessions?" they say. "What kind of life will that be, selling everything, being dispossessed of everything?" Don't ask me for the rationale of the Master's commandments. He who lays down the law knows how to bring even what is incapable into accordance with the law. But as for you, your heart is tested as on a balance, to see if it shall incline towards the true life or towards immediate gratification. For it is right for those who are prudent in their reasonings to regard the use of money as a matter of stewardship, not of selfish enjoyment; and those who lay it aside ought to rejoice as though separated from things alien, not be embittered as though deprived of what is nearest and dearest. So why become depressed? Why are you so sick at heart, when you hear the words, "Sell your possessions"? For if, on the one hand, these possessions could follow you into the afterlife, they should not therefore be highly valued, when next to the prizes that await there they should be thrown into the shade . . .

"For where your treasure is, there will your heart be also."

4. What answer shall you make to the judge, you who dress walls, but will not clothe a man; who spruce up horses, and overlook an unfashionable brother; who leave grain to rot, but will not feed the starving; who bury your money and despise the oppressed? And truly, if you dwell with a covetous wife, the sickness is redoubled: she turns up the flame on luxuries, she multiplies hedonisms, and provokes overactive longings, while she sets her fancy upon various stones: pearls, and emeralds, and sapphires; as also gold, some forged, some woven: aggravating the disease with every form of bad taste. For it's not a part-time occupation, these concerns, but night and day are caught up in their cares. And a thousand parasites, worming themselves in via these lusts, bring in the dyers, goldsmiths, perfumers, weavers, embroiderers. They give a man no time to breathe, by reason of his wife's continual demands . . .

Accordingly, when a man and his wife drag their wealth about, this way and that, to such ends, winning each other over in the discovering of vanities, no wonder the wealth hasn't the opportunity to stoop aside to other people. When you hear it said, "Sell your possessions, and give to the poor," so that you might have provisions for heavenly enjoyment, you go away grieving; but if you should hear, "Give money for pampering your wife, give to stonemasons, carpenters, mosaic pebble-layers, portrait-painters," you rejoice as though you had acquired some high-rated annuities.

Do you see these walls here, broken down by time, whose remnants, like watchtowers, peer out across the length of the city? How many paupers were there in town when these were being raised, who, because of the attention given to such things, were ignored by the wealthy of that day? Where then is now the wonderful monument of their labors, and where is the man who devoted himself to such great works? Isn't the one now buried and dissolved, like sandcastles children love to build, while the other lies in hell, regretting his care for nullities? Let your heart be big: but as for walls, both small and large fulfill the same function.

When I enter the house of a man who is tasteless and nouveau-riche[3], and see it shimmering with every kind of flowery crass trinket, I apprehend that this man has acquired nothing more valuable in his life than visible things, but, while he gives what is soulless a facelift, he possesses an unbeautified soul. Tell me, what better service do silver beds and silver tables, ivory sofas and ivory chairs provide, when because of these things wealth fails to pass over to the poor, and thousands huddle about the door, all of them letting loose a miserable howl? You, however, refuse to give, declaring that it's impossible to satisfy those who ask. With your tongue you excuse yourself, but by your own hand you're convicted; for even in silence your hand proclaims your falsehood, sparkling round from the ring on your finger. How many people could one of your fingers release from debt? How many broken-down homes could be rebuilt? One box of your clothing would be able to dress the whole shivering populace; but you, unfeeling, dismiss the needy, not fearing the just repayment of the Judge. You have not shown mercy, you shall not receive mercy; you've not opened your home, you shall be evicted from the

---

3   Nouveau-riche – newly rich

kingdom. You haven't given of your bread; neither shall you receive eternal life.

5. "But I'm poor!" you say, and I'll vouch for you. For he is poor who lacks much. And much are you lacking, because of unfulfillable desire. To ten talents you seek to add another ten, and when there are twenty, you seek to add so many more; and always the addition, far from putting the urge to rest, whets the appetite. For just as with alcoholics a fresh bottle of wine becomes an excuse for drinking, so also those who are recently grown rich, and have acquired great possessions, desire more of the same, nursing the sickness with perpetual addition; and in their love they are carried to opposites . . . They ought to be happy and contented, being well-off in so much; but they bear it ill and are pained that they still fall short of one or two of the super-rich. When they catch up with this tycoon, immediately they yearn to be made equal to somebody richer; and if they outdo him, the desire is transferred to another. Just as those who climb a ladder lift their foot always one step above and do not stop till they've reached the top, in the same way these people do not cease from their drive for power, till, having risen very high, a fall from their sublimity dashes them to the ground . . .

So much as the eye sees, so much does the covetous man desire. "The eye is not filled with seeing" (Eccl 1:8), and the money-lover is not satisfied with getting. "Hell does not say, Enough" (Prov 27:20; 30:16); neither does the covetous man ever say, Enough. When will you make use of your present things? When will you enjoy them, you who are forever involved in a struggle to acquire? "Woe unto them that join house to house, that lay field to field,"

so that they may take from their neighbor (Isa 5:8). But
what do you do? Don't you seek a thousand quarrels, in
order to take what belongs to your neighbor? My
neighbor's house, they say, blocks the sunlight; they make
too much noise; they hold strange views; or on the grounds
of some other chance accusation, you harass them, and
kick them out, and drag them into court, and hound them,
never ceasing till you have succeeded in turning them
into vagabonds . . .

6. I would like you to take a short vacation from works
of iniquity, and give your calculations a rest, so that you
might seriously consider the kind of end towards which
these preoccupations are heading. You have such and such
an amount of arable land, and of wooded land so much
more: hills, plains, valleys, rivers, streams. What, then,
comes next? Don't six feet of earth, in all, await you?
Won't the weight of a few stones suffice to keep your
weary flesh? What is it that you toil over? To what end
do you work iniquity? Why do your hands glean a thing
that yields no fruit? Yes, and if only it were merely fruitless,
and not also fuel for eternal fire! Will you never sober up
from this intoxication? never heal your reasonings? never
come to yourself? Won't you set before your eyes the
judgment seat of Christ? What will you have to say for
yourself, when there shall stand about you in a circle
those you have wronged, all of them crying against you
before the righteous Judge? What will you do? What
lawyers will you bribe? What witnesses will you produce?
How will you corrupt that wholly undeceivable Judge?
You'll find no slick talker there, no verbal spin, to steal
the strength of the Judge of truth. No lackeys follow
you, nor money, nor dignity of place; deserted by friends,
deserted of helpers, without an advocate, without

defense, you will be left utterly ashamed, abashed, dejected, abandoned, speechless. For all around, in whatever direction you turn your gaze, you clearly see the images of your misdeeds: here the tears of orphans, there a widow's groanings, elsewhere the poor you stepped on, servants you tore to shreds, neighbors you enraged: all will withstand you; the wicked choir of your evil deeds will tangle you in snares . . .

7. . . . People, what's the matter with you? Who has done this to you, to turn your things into a conspiracy against you? "I need them for my life-style." Well, and hasn't your money furnished provisions for wrongdoing? "It's a form of insurance." Isn't it rather a means of self-destruction? "But money's a necessity, on account of the children." A fine excuse for greed: you parade your kids, but gratify your own desires. I do not accuse the innocent man: he has his Master, and his responsibilities; from another he received life, from himself he finds means of staying alive. But wasn't this Gospel passage written also for married folk: "If you want to be perfect, sell your belongings, and give to the poor" (Matt 19:21)? When you asked the Lord for a large family, when you prayed that you might be a father of children, did you then add the following: "Give me children, so that I may ignore your commandments. Give me children, so that I might not attain to the kingdom of heaven"?

And who will guarantee you of your child's intentions, that what you give will be rightly used? For wealth turns out to be, for many people, a minister of impurity. Or don't you hear Ecclesiastes, who says, "I have seen a sore malaise, riches kept in store for one who comes after a man, to his hurt" (Eccl 5:13). And again, "I left it for the

man who should come after me. And who knows if
he shall be a wise man or a fool?" (Eccl 2:18-19). See to
this, then, lest, having accumulated your wealth through
countless pains, you prepare it for others as material for
sins, and then find yourself doubly punished, both for
what you did yourself, and for the means you gave to others.
Doesn't your own soul belong to you more intimately
than any child? Isn't it joined to you by a more intimate
closeness than anything else? Give to it the first privileges
of inheritance, provide it with a richer living; and afterwards
distribute to your children what they need to get by in
life. Often it happens that children who have received
nothing from their parents have gone on to establish estates
for themselves; but as for your soul, if you don't take care
of it, who will pity it?

8. So much for fathers: what's been said has been said.
Now, what plausible causes of stinginess shall the childless
fling at us? "I don't sell my possessions, neither give to
the poor, on account of life's necessities." Therefore the
Lord is not your teacher, neither does the Gospel direct
your life, but you are yourself your own lawgiver. See into
what a danger you fall, when reasoning like this. For if
the Lord has ordered these things as necessary to you, and
you, for your part, write them off as impossible, you say
nothing less than that you yourself are more intelligent than
the Lawgiver. "But," you say, "after I've enjoyed these
things all my days, when my life is over I will cause the
poor to inherit the things I formerly possessed, and in
a written testament I will declare them to be the owners."
When you no longer exist among human beings, then
you become a lover of humanity. When I see you dead,
then I shall be able to say that you love your brother.

A great many thanks to you for this noble gesture, that, when you are lying in the tomb, and decomposing into earth, then you grow substantial with spending, and become big-hearted. Tell me, which years will you be looking to receive wages for, those during your life, or those when you're dead? But when you were alive you passed your time wallowing in life's luxuries, floating along with your delicacies, and wouldn't bear to cast a glance to the poor. When you die, then, what sort of action is ascribed to you? What sort of wage is owed you for labor? Show the works, then ask for the returns. Nobody does business after the market closes, neither after the games end does anyone come up to be crowned, neither after a war does anyone prove his valor. Neither, then, is godliness to be postponed till after life, as is obvious.

Again, you promise to write up your benefactions in black and white. So who shall announce to you the time of your departure? Who will be your actuary, to guarantee the mode of your death? How many have been snatched away in violent accidents, not even able to let go a cry in their pains? How many have been made delirious by fever? Why then do you wait for a time when you may no longer be in command of your faculties? The night is deep, the sickness is crushing, and there is no one to help; and he who sits by, waiting for an inheritance, is ready to manipulate everything towards his own profit, turning all your intentions to no purpose.

At that time, turning your gaze here and there, and seeing the void that surrounds you, you will perceive your foolishness: then you will groan for the mindlessness you showed in putting off the commandment, at that hour when your tongue lies slack, and your trembling hand is jerked by spasms, since neither by voice nor in writing shall you be able to indicate your intent. And indeed, even if you've written everything clearly, and have expressly declared all things by voice, a single letter interpolated into the text suffices to change its meaning: one counterfeit seal, two or three false witnesses, and the whole inheritance is passed over to others.

9. Why then do you deceive yourself, misusing wealth now for carnal enjoyment, and promising for the future things which will no longer be under your control? As this sermon has shown, it is an evil counsel that says: Living, I'll enjoy my pleasures; dead, I'll do what's been commanded. Abraham also says to you, "You received your good things during your life" (Luke 16:25). The narrow, straightened way does not admit you, since you haven't put off the bulkiness of your wealth. You departed still carrying it; you didn't toss it aside, as you'd been directed. While you lived, you set yourself above the commandment; after death and decomposition, then you value the commandment above your enemies . . . So death deserves the thanks, not you. For if you were immortal, you would never have remembered the commandments . . . Dead things are not brought to a sacrificial altar: bring forth a living sacrifice. Unacceptable is the one who makes an offering from his superfluity. But in your case, those things you had in excess all your life are what you present to your benefactor. If you dare not welcome honorable men to your home with kitchen leftovers, how dare you offer leftovers to appease God?

Consider then the end of covetousness, you who are rich, and cease from your passionate affection towards legal tender. However much you adore wealth, to that very extent you should rather leave not one thing behind that belongs to you. You want everything to be your own, you want to bring everything with you. But possibly your own servants will not clothe you for the world to come, but will skimp on your burial, cheerfully bestowing the savings upon your inheritors. Or perhaps they will philosophize against you then: "How tasteless and inappropriate," they'll say, "to beautify a corpse, and to give expensive burial to someone who can no longer perceive. What? should we not in fact accessorize present company with expensive, swanky apparel, rather than bury a dead person's most valuable garments along with him? What good is a monument over the grave, and a pompous burial, and useless expenditure? It is right that things needful for life be made use of by the living." Such things they'll say, getting back at you for your meanness, and using your effects to ingratiate themselves with your heirs.

Get a head start on them, then. Prepare your own self for burial. Piety makes a lovely winding-sheet. Come away fully dressed: make wealth your peculiar beauty. Take it with you. Believe in the good counsel, in Christ who loves you, who for us became poor, so that through his poverty we might become rich, who gave himself as a ransom for us. Whether, then, because, as he is wise, he immediately sees what is helpful to us, let us trust in him; or because he loves us, let us pray to him; or because he does us good, let us do good in turn. And let us, in any case, do the things he has directed us to do, so that we may become inheritors of the everlasting life which is in the same Christ, to whom be glory and power, world without end. Amen.

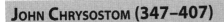

JOHN CHRYSOSTOM (347–407)

Background

The name *Chrysostom* means *golden-mouthed*. John's eloquence and skill in preaching earned him the name *John of the Golden-Mouth*. He was trained in the Antiochene School, which encouraged him toward more literal interpretations of the commands of Jesus rather than the comparatively figurative interpretations of Alexandria (like Clement's). Additionally, whereas the Alexandrian School stressed the union of divine and human natures in Jesus, the Antiochene School stressed the importance of the distinction between the natures. Both, however, agreed that Jesus was fully God and fully man and rejected heretical[4] ways of thinking about Jesus that diminished either his divinity or his humanity.

Chrysostom eventually became bishop of Constantinople[5]. He undertook reforms in the church, including refusing the luxuries of the bishop's estate and calling church leaders to live simply. He also reemphasized caring for the poor and widows. From the money he saved by rejecting luxury, he started a hospital for those in need. He regularly positioned himself against wealthy patrons and on the side of people in poverty who were being abused or oppressed. While he was respected as a church leader, his rebuke of several people in power eventually led to his exile, where he died. However, the body of this much-loved pastor was brought back to Constantinople for his burial with great fanfare.

---

4   Heretical – unhealthy

5   Constantinople – modern-day Istanbul

Chrysostom is often considered one of the greatest preachers of the Christian tradition. In this sermon, he chooses as his text the parable of the rich man and Lazarus, a choice that will be echoed by many other thinkers down through the ages as they preach on Christian mission and poverty.

Text

Second Discourse on Luke 16:19–31:
The Parable of the Rich Man and Lazarus

1. I was pleased yesterday to see your right feeling when I entered upon the subject of Lazarus, inasmuch as you approved of the patience of the poor man, and shrank from the cruelty and inhumanity of the rich man. These are no small tokens of a noble mind. For if, though not possessing virtue, we yet praise it, then we may be at all events more able to attain it. In like manner if, though we do not flee from sin, we still blame sin, then we may at all events be able to escape from it. Since, therefore, you received that address with great favor, let me deliver to you those things which still remain.

You then saw Lazarus in the gateway of the rich man; today behold him in Abraham's bosom. You saw him then licked by dogs; see him now guarded and tended by angels. You saw him then in poverty; behold him now in affluence. You saw him wanting food; behold him enjoying the greatest plenty. You saw him engaged in the contest; behold him crowned as victor. You saw his labor; behold his reward; behold it, whether you be rich or poor—if rich, that you may not think highly of wealth apart from virtue—if poor, that you may not think poverty, in itself, an evil. To both classes this man may afford instruction. If he, living in poverty, did not resent his lot, what excuse will they have who do so in wealth? If, living in want and amid so many ills, he could give thanks, what defense can they make who, while they possess abundance, have no desire to attain to the virtue of thankfulness?

Again; those who are poor, and who on that account are vexed and discontented, what excuse can they have, when this man, who lived in continual hunger and poverty, desertion and weakness, and who passed his days hard by the dwelling of a rich man; who was scorned by all, while there was no one else who had suffered the like, to whom he might look, still showed such patience and resignation? From him we may learn not to think the rich happy nor the poor miserable. Or rather, to speak the truth, he is not rich who is surrounded by many possessions, but he who does not *need* many possessions; and he is not poor who possesses nothing, but he who requires many things. We ought to consider this to be the distinction between poverty and wealth.

When, therefore, you see any one longing for many things, esteem him of all men the poorest, even though he possess all manner of wealth; again, when you see one who does not wish for many things, judge him to be of all men most affluent, even if he possess nothing. For by the condition of our mind, not by the quantity of our material wealth, should it be our custom to distinguish between poverty and affluence . . . For he who cannot restrain his desires, even if he should be surrounded by every kind of possessions, how can he ever be rich? Those, indeed, who are satisfied with their own property, enjoying what they have, and not casting a covetous eye on the substance of others, even if they be, as to means, of all men the most limited, ought to be regarded as the most affluent. For he who does not desire other people's possessions, but is willing to be satisfied with his own, is the wealthiest of all.

However, with your permission, let us return to the proposed subject. "It came to pass," it is said, "that Lazarus died; and he was carried up by angels" (Luke 16:22) . . .

2. . . . Not the souls of the just only, but also those of sinners are led away. This also is clear from the case of another rich man. For when his land brought forth abundantly, he said within himself, "What shall I do? I will pull down my barns and build greater" (Luke 12:18). Than this state of mind nothing could be more wretched. He did in truth pull down his barns; for secure storehouses are not built with walls of stone; they are "the mouths of the poor." But this man neglecting these, was busy about stone walls. What, however, did God say to him? *"You fool, this night shall they require your soul of you."*

3. You are silent as you listen to these things. Much rather would I have silence than applause. Applause and praises tend to my own glory; but silence tends to make you wiser. I know that what has been said causes pain, but it brings also great and inexpressible advantage. That rich man, if he had had someone to admonish him of these things, and had not had those flatterers counseling him always with a view to favor, and encouraging him in luxury, would not have come to the place of punishment; he would not have endured those insupportable tortures, he would not afterwards have repented so inconsolably. But

since all his associates spoke with a view to favor, they betrayed him to the fire . . .

Beloved, do not carelessly pass by this word "he was buried"; but let us think of the tables inlaid with silver, the couches, the carpets, the vestments, all the ornaments throughout the house, the unguents, the perfumes, the abundance of wine, the variety of meats, the confections, the cooks, the flatterers, the attendants, the household slaves, and all the rest of the display, all burnt up and come to nothing. All is ashes, all cinders and dust, lamentations and mourning; no one any longer able to help him, or to bring back the departing soul. *Then* was made manifest the real power of gold, and of all the rest of his wealth. From all that crowd of attendants, he departed naked and alone, not being able out of all that abundance to carry anything away; but he went away destitute and deserted. No one of all his servants, no one of his supporters was at hand to rescue him from punishment, but led away from all these, he is alone taken to bear those insupportable penalties. Truly "all flesh is as grass, and all the glory thereof as the flower of grass. The grass withers, and the flower fades; but the word of the Lord abides forever" (Isa 40:6, 7).

Death came and withered all those things, and seizing the man himself as a captive, led him away downcast, filled with shame, speechless, trembling, afraid; him who had, as in a dream, enjoyed all that luxury. And after this, the rich man became a suppliant of the poor man, and required a supply from the table of him who once was famishing, and who lay at his gate, licked by dogs. Affairs were now reversed. All men now learned which was the rich man and which the poor, and that Lazarus was one of the most wealthy of men, and the rich man one of the most destitute . . .

Thus it often happens, that one of those who are here the most wealthy, is there most poor, as it was also in the case of this rich man. For when evening, that is, death, came, and he went out from the theatre of the present life, and put off his mask, he was seen there to be poorest of all, even so poor as not to possess a drop of water, but obliged to beg for this, and not gain the object of his petition. What could be more abject than poverty like this? And hear how having lifted up his eyes, he said to Abraham, "Father, have mercy on me and send Lazarus, that he may dip the tip of his finger in water and cool my tongue" (Luke 16:24). Do you see how great his tribulation is? Him whom he passed by when he was close at hand, he now calls to when far off; him upon whom he often, in going out and coming in, did not bestow a glance, he now, when far off, regards steadfastly.

But why does he now look at him? Very often, perhaps, the rich man had said, "What need have I of piety and goodness? All things flow to me as from a perennial fountain. I enjoy great honor, great prosperity. I suffer no unwished-for casualty. Why should I strive after goodness? This poor man, though he lives in piety and goodness, suffers a thousand ills." Many in these days often say such things. In order, therefore, that these false notions might be completely rooted out, it is shown to the rich man, that for wickedness there is in store punishment, and for righteous toil, a crown and honor. And not only on this account did the rich man then see the poor man, but also that the rich man should endure the same that the poor man had endured, and in a higher degree.

As therefore, in the case of the poor man, his being laid at the gate of the rich man, and thus seeing the prosperity of another, had made his affliction much heavier, thus also, in the case of the rich man, it made his pain greater, that he, now lying in the place of punishment, also sees the bliss of Lazarus; so that, not only by the very nature of torture, but by the contrast with the other's honor, he should bear more insufferable punishment . . . "I sent to you," He might say, "this poor man Lazarus to your gate, that he might be to you a teacher of virtue, and an opportunity for the exercise of benevolence. You did overlook the gain; you were not willing to use aright this means of salvation. From henceforth find it to be a cause of increased pain and punishment."

We learn from this that all those whom we have despitefully treated or wronged will then meet us face to face. Still this man was not in any way *wronged* by the rich man: for the rich man did not seize any of his property; yet he bestowed not upon him any of his own. And since he did not bestow anything on him, he had the neglected poor man for his accuser. What mercy can he expect who has robbed other men's goods, when he is surrounded by all those whom he has injured! No need is there of witnesses, none of accusers, none of evidences or proofs; but the very deeds themselves, whatsoever we have committed, will then be placed before our own eyes.

Behold, then, it is said, the man and his works. This also is robbery—not to impart our good things to others. Very likely it may seem to you a strange saying; but wonder not at it, for I will, from the Divine Scriptures, bring testimony showing that not only robbery of other men's goods, but also the not imparting our own good things to others—that this also is robbery, and covetousness, and fraud. What then is this testimony? God, rebuking the Jews, speaks thus through the prophet: "The earth has brought forth her fruit, and you have not brought in the tithes; but the plunder of the poor is in your houses" (Mal 3:10). Since, it is said, you have not given the customary oblations, you have robbed the poor. This is said in order to show to the rich that they possess things which belong to the poor, even if their property be gained by inheritance—in fact, from whatever source their substance be derived.

And, again, in another place, it is said, "Do not deprive the poor of life" (Ecclus[6] 4:1). Now, he who *deprives*, deprives some other man of property. It is said to be deprivation when we retain things taken from others. And in this way, therefore, we are taught that if we do not bestow alms, we shall be treated in the same way as those who have been extortioners. Our Lord's things they are, from wherever we may obtain them. And if we distribute to the needy we shall obtain for ourselves great abundance.

And for this it is that God has permitted you to possess much—not that you should spend it in fornication, in drunkenness, in gluttony, in rich clothing, or any other mode of luxury, but that you should distribute it to the needy. And just as if a receiver of taxes, having in charge the king's property, should not distribute it to those for whom it is ordered, but should spend it for his own

---

6   Ecclesiasticus – a book in the Apocrypha, a collection of writings between the Old and New Testaments that is included in the Roman Catholic Bible.

enjoyment, he would pay the penalty and come to ruin; thus also the rich man is, as it were, a receiver of goods which are destined to be dispensed to the poor—to those of his fellow-servants who are in want. If he then should spend upon himself more than he really needs, he will pay hereafter a heavy penalty. For the things he has are not his own, but are the things of his fellow-servants.

4. Let us then be as sparing of our possessions as we should be of those of other people, that they may become really our own. In what manner, then, can we be as sparing of them as of those of other people? By not expending them on superfluous wants, nor for our own needs only, but by imparting them also to the poor. Even if you are a rich man, if you spend more than you need, you will render an account of the property which has been entrusted to you. This same thing happens in great households. Many in this way entrust their entire property into the hands of dependents; yet those who are thus trusted take care of the things delivered to them, and do not squander the deposit, but distribute to whomever and whenever the master orders. The same thing do you. If you have received more than others, you have received it, not that you only should spend it, but that you should be a good steward of it for the advantage of others . . .

The same thing also St Paul[7] with much admiration insists on, in these words: "Be not forgetful to entertain strangers; for thereby some have entertained angels unawares" (Heb 13:2). And well does he say unawares . . . For if they had knowingly received them with such goodwill, they would have done no great or wonderful

---

7   Some early Christians held Paul to be the author of Hebrews.

thing: all the praise depends on the fact that not knowing who they were that passed by, and supposing them to be simply wayfaring men, they with such alacrity invited them to enter. If when you receive some noble and honorable man you display such zeal as this, you do nothing wonderful; for the nobility of the guest obliges even the inhospitable often to show all kindness. It is this that is great and admirable—that when they are chance guests, wanderers, people of limited means, we receive them with great goodwill. Thus also Christ, speaking of those who acted thus, said: "Inasmuch as you have done it unto one of the least of these, you have done it unto Me" (Matt 25:45) . . .

Since Abraham also was wise in this respect, he did not inquire of travelers as to who they were, or from whence they came, as we do in these days; but he simply received all who passed by. It becomes him that is truly well-disposed not to require an account of a man's past life, but simply to relieve poverty and to satisfy want. The poor man has only one plea—his poverty, and his being in want. Demand from him nothing more; but if he be the most wicked of all, and be in need of necessary food, you ought to satisfy his hunger. Thus did Christ command us to do, when he said, "Be you like your Father which is in heaven, for He makes His sun to shine on the evil and on the good, and sends rain on the just and on the unjust" (Matt 5:45).

The merciful man is as a harbor to those who are in need; and the harbor receives all who are escaping shipwreck, and frees them from danger, whether they be evil or good; whatsoever kind of men they be that are in peril, it receives them into its shelter. You also, when you see a man suffering shipwreck on land through poverty, do not sit in judgment on him, nor require explanations, but relieve his distress. Why do you give yourself unnecessary trouble? God frees you from all such anxiety and labor. How many things would many men have said, and how many difficulties would they have caused, if God had commanded us to inquire accurately into a man's life, his antecedents, the things which each man had previously done; and after this, to have pity on him!

But now are we free from all this trouble. "Why, then, do we burden ourselves with superfluous cares? To be a judge is one thing, to be merciful is another. Mercy is called by that name for this reason, that it gives even to the unworthy. This again St Paul teaches, when he says, "Be not weary in doing good, indeed to all, but especially unto them that are of the household of faith" (Gal 6:10). If we are concerned and troubled about keeping the unworthy away, it will not be likely that the worthy come within our reach; but if we impart to the unworthy, also the worthy—even those who are so worthy as to counterbalance all the rest—will assuredly come under our influence. In this way it befell Abraham, of blessed memory, who, not troubling himself nor being inquisitive about these wayfarers, was once privileged to entertain even angels. Him let us zealously imitate . . .

5. Thus, I beseech you, let us also do, not making a more minute inquiry than is necessary. For the need of the poor man is a sufficient cause of itself; and whosoever with this qualification should at any time come to us, let us not trouble ourselves further; for we do not minister to the character, but to the man: we have pity on him, not on account of his virtue, but on account of his calamity, in order that we also may gain that great mercy from the Lord—that we also, though unworthy, may gain His

favor. For if we seek for worthiness in our fellow-servants, and make diligent inquiry, the same also will God do to us; and if we demand explanations from our fellow-servants, we ourselves shall fail to gain favor from above. "With what judgment," it is said, "you judge, you shall be judged" (Matt 8:2).

But let us again turn our discourse to the subject on hand. Seeing this poor man, therefore, in the bosom of Abraham, the rich man said, "Father Abraham, have mercy on me, and send Lazarus." Why does he not address his words to Lazarus? It seems to me that he was ashamed and daunted, and that he thought that Lazarus would assuredly retain an angry remembrance of the things done to him . . . We do not say this to disparage Lazarus; for he was not at all thus disposed—far from it; but the rich man, fearing such things as this, did not address him, but raised his voice to Abraham, whom he might suppose to be ignorant of what had happened. And now he strove to gain the service of that finger which he had often allowed to be licked by dogs.

What then did Abraham say to him? "Son! you in your lifetime received your good things" (Luke 16:25). Mark the wisdom—mark the tenderness of the saint! He did not say, "Inhuman and cruel man! full of all wickedness! Having inflicted such evils on this man, do you now speak of benevolence, or pity, or compassion! Do you not blush! Are you not ashamed!" But what does he say? "Son," he says, "you received your good things." For it is also written, "You shall not add trouble to an afflicted soul" (Ecclus 4:3). The trouble which he has brought upon himself is sufficient . . . Why also did he not say "you had," but "you received"? Here I perceive a vast sea of thought opening out before us.

Therefore, keeping in mind with all care the things which have been already said, as well those now said as those yesterday, let us safely store them in the mind. By means of that which has been said, make yourselves better prepared to hear that which will be spoken on another occasion, and, if possible, remember all that has been said; and if that be not possible, I beg that, chief of all, you will remember constantly that not to share our own riches with the poor is a robbery of the poor, and a depriving them of their livelihood; and that that which we possess is not only our own, but also theirs. If our minds are disposed in accordance with this truth, we shall freely use all our possessions; we shall feed Christ while hungering here, and we shall lay up great treasures there; we shall be enabled to attain future blessedness, by the grace and favor of our Lord, with whom, to the Father and the Holy Spirit, be glory, honor, might, now and ever, even to all eternity. Amen.

Discussion Questions

 Basil and Chrysostom see people in their communities living in wealth while others live in poverty. Do you see this in your own neighborhood, community, or country? What do Basil and Chrysostom think Christians should do about this reality?

 In what ways do Basil and Chrysostom interpret Jesus' commands to the rich young man differently than the way Clement interprets them? Are there any similarities between their opinions about wealth?

 Basil seems to talk about the idea of having enough. Are you content with what you have?

 Why would Chrysostom say that refusing to give to the poor is robbery? Are there ways you are refusing to use your hands for the benefit of people who are marginalized?

 Basil is fairly critical of people spending money on décor and fancy clothing. He also has concerns about people saving for their children instead of giving. Are there practices you are engaging in that detract from God's mission among the poor?

Chapter 4

Holy Poverty

O blessed poverty, that provides eternal riches to those who love and embrace it!

O holy poverty, God promises the kingdom of heaven and, of course, gives eternal glory and a happy life to those who possess and desire it!

O noble poverty, that the Lord Jesus Christ, who ruled and is ruling heaven and earth, and who spoke and all things were made, chose to embrace before anything else!

~ Clare of Assisi

And if you would see him humiliated and in great poverty, look at God made man, clothed in the lowliness of your humanity . . .

At the end of his life . . . he was so poor on the wood of
the cross that neither the earth nor the wood could give
him a place to lay his head. He had nowhere to rest it
except on his own shoulder.

~ Catherine of Siena

CLARE OF ASSISI (1194–1253)

Background

Clare was born to a wealthy family of nobles in Assisi in
what is now the country of Italy. Destined to be married to
another noble or a ruler for the economic power that such
an alliance would provide, Clare saw the ways in which
money and land rights were used to keep others poor. She
learned of another child of wealth who had forsaken his
inheritance to live among the poor, a young monk named
Francis. Because many medieval monasteries were rich and
powerful and were involved in the very land conflicts that
displaced people who were poor, Francis had petitioned
the Pope to allow him to start a new religious order. As
a woman in the medieval west, Clare could not start her
own religious order. But she could seek solace and
protection from the Franciscans, the monastic order that
followed Francis. She fled the violence, wealth, and
debased sexuality of the noble class to live a life devoted
to God and the pursuit of poverty and chastity.

While Francis of Assisi has now become a household
name, it was Clare who more fully understood how power
and money were aligned in ways that destroyed people.

Whereas Francis was heir to a wealthy merchant family, Clare was born of nobility, with the political knowledge it entailed. Whereas Francis had received the call to reform the church through the pursuit of poverty, Clare realized that the pursuit of poverty was the only way to resist the decadence and greed of her times. Recognizing how political and economic systems and structures often worked to devalue the inherent dignity of the poor, she formed a friendship with Agnes of Prague, the daughter of Hungarian royalty who was destined to marry Frederick II, king of Germany and eventual Holy Roman Emperor. Agnes had rejected her political marriage and had used her fortune to found a hospital and a monastery. She then requested that Clare send monastic sisters from the Franciscan order to help and Clare obliged. Clare and Agnes carried on a correspondence of which several letters have survived.

We may be confused today by Clare's praise of poverty as holy, but Clare understood that only by standing in solidarity with the poor and committing herself to chastity could she resist the principalities and powers that stood in opposition to the Gospel. Francis and Clare took Jesus' command to the rich young ruler as a literal command to them. In so doing, they provided an alternative to the alignment of political power and church power. It was the good news of the Gospel for the poor that propelled them to obey Jesus in this way. As you read Clare's first letter to Agnes, pay attention to how she understands Christian mission as God's embrace of the poor.

Text

First Letter to Agnes of Prague

To Lady Agnes, venerable and most holy virgin, daughter of the most renowned and illustrious king of Bohemia, Clare, her subject and handmaid in all circumstances, an unworthy servant of Jesus Christ and the useless handmaid of the enclosed ladies of the Monastery of San Damiano, commends herself in every way and send, with special respect, the wish that Agnes attain the glory of everlasting happiness.

Hearing the news, which brings you the highest honor, of your holy conversion and manner of life—news that has been reputably disseminated not only to me but to nearly every region of the world—I rejoice and exalt exceedingly in the Lord. Concerning this news, I am not the only one who rejoices, but I am joined by all those who serve and desire to serve Jesus Christ.

I rejoice because you, more than others—having had the opportunity to become legitimately married with eminent glory to the illustrious emperor as would befit your and his pre-eminence—could have enjoyed public ostentation, honors, and worldly status. Spurning all these things with your whole heart and mind, you have chosen instead holiest poverty and physical want, accepting a nobler spouse, the Lord Jesus Christ, who will keep your virginity always immaculate and inviolable.

> Having loved him, you are chaste;
>
> Having touched him, you will be made pure;
>
> Having received him, you are a virgin.

His power is stronger,

His nobility higher,

His appearance lovelier,

His love sweeter,

And his grace more elegant.

You are now held tightly in the embrace

Of the one

Who has adorned your breast with precious stones

And has hung priceless pearls from your ears.

He has completely covered you with

Glittering and sparkling gems,

And has placed on your head a golden crown

Engraved with the seal of holiness.

Therefore, dearest sister—or should I say, most venerable lady, because you are spouse and mother and sister of my Lord Jesus Christ, and are most resplendently distinguished by the banner of inviolable virginity and holiest poverty—be strengthened in the holy service begun in you out of a burning desire for the Poor Crucified. For all of us he endured the passion of the cross, rescuing us from the power of the prince of darkness—by whose power we were kept in chains because of the transgression of our first parent—and reconciling us to God the Father.

O blessed poverty

That provides eternal riches to those who

Love and embrace it!

> O holy poverty,
> God promises the kingdom of heaven
> And, of course,
> Gives eternal glory and a happy life
> To those who possess and desire it!
> O noble poverty
> That the Lord Jesus Christ, who ruled
> And is ruling heaven and earth,
> And who spoke and all things were made,
> Chose to embrace before anything else!

For foxes have dens, scripture says, and the birds of the sky have nests, but the Son of Man, who is Christ, has nowhere to lay his head; instead, bowing his head, he handed over his spirit.

If, then, such a great Lord when coming into the virgin's womb chose to appear contemptible, needy, and poor in this world so that human beings, who were utterly poor and needy, suffering from a dire lack of heavenly food, might be made rich in him by means of the kingdom of heaven that they will indeed possess, exalt exceedingly and rejoice, filled with great joy and spiritual happiness. Because—since contempt of the world has pleased you more than its honors; poverty more than temporal riches; and storing up treasures in heaven rather than on earth where neither rust consumes them, nor moth destroys them, and thieves do not dig them up and steal them— your most abundant reward is in heaven, and you have quite fittingly deserved to be called sister, spouse, and

"For foxes have dens, and the birds of the sky have nests,
but the Son of Man has nowhere to lay his head."

mother of the Son of the Most High Father and the glorious Virgin.[1]

For, I am sure that you know that the kingdom of heaven is promised and given by the Lord only to the poor, because as long as something temporal is the object of love, the fruit of charity is lost. You know, too, that a person cannot serve God and material wealth, since either the one is loved and the other hated, or the person will serve one and despise the other. You also know that a person wearing clothing cannot fight with another who is naked, because the one who has something that might be grasped is more quickly thrown to the ground.

You also know that it is not possible for a person to remain glorious in the world and to reign with Christ in heaven; and that a camel will be able to pass through the eye of a needle before a rich person ascends into the kingdom of heaven. These are the reasons why you disposed of your clothing, I mean your worldly wealth, so that you might have the strength not to succumb completely to the one struggling against you, and might enter the kingdom of heaven by the narrow road and constricted gate.

> It is indeed a great and praiseworthy exchange
>
> To give up the temporal for the eternal,
>
> To merit the heavenly rather than the earthly,
>
> To receive a hundredfold instead of one,
>
> To have a happy, everlasting life.

---

1   Virgin – a reference to Mary, whom Roman Catholics hold in high regard as the mother of Jesus.

Given that you want to be strengthened in his holy service growing from good to better, from virtue to virtue, I thought, therefore, that I should do all I can to implore Your Excellency and Holiness with humble prayers in the innermost heart of Christ, so that the one to whose service you devote yourself with every desire of your mind may choose to bestow freely upon you the rewards you have desired.

I also beseech you in the Lord, as best as I can, to be so kind as to include in your most holy prayers me, your servant, although useless, and the other sisters who are devoted to you who live with me in the monastery. By the help of your prayers, may we be able to merit the mercy of Jesus Christ so that we, together with you, may deserve to enjoy the everlasting vision.

Farewell in the Lord, and please pray for me.

CATHERINE OF SIENA (1347–1380)

Background

Catherine of Siena, much like Clare of Assisi, had to fight the life planned for her by her family and society—arranged marriage—in order to live a life of ministry. At the age of eighteen she joined a Dominican monastery only to later return to living outside the monastery in order to care for the poor and sick in homes and hospitals. She is often called a "social mystic" or a "mystic activist"[2] because of her combination of contemplation and action. During her brief life she was a monastic, an advisor to popes, a skilled

---

2 Noffke, *Catherine of Siena: The Dialogue*, 9.

theologian and author, a political advocate, and a caregiver for people on the margins. She often put her own health at risk by her service to others and severe fasting. Yet this single-minded, almost obsessive devotion also opened her to receive dramatic revelations from God. Alongside these revelations, her theological acumen earned her the title of "doctor" of the Roman Catholic Church.

Much like other medieval women theologians, including Julian of Norwich, Catherine phrased her writings as God speaking to her and her responding to God (hence the title *The Dialogue*). While she received mystical, ecstatic visions of God, she was also a skilled writer and astute thinker. One wonders if, in addition to the special revelations she received from Christ, Catherine was aware that as a woman her ideas might be better received if she didn't present them as her own. Either way, we see in Catherine a similar combination of prayer and work that we have seen in several other thinkers.

In this reading, Catherine makes a distinction between the general commandments given to all Christians and the special counsels given to those who would lead a single life of religious devotion. While the Protestant Reformation would later push back against this two-tiered distinction of calling (and in its place offer the priesthood of all believers), Catherine's distinguishing of commands and counsels points to an important idea. Catherine goes to great lengths to explain why those committed to family life may interpret the ideal of poverty in a more figurative sense while those committed to celibacy in ministry may interpret the ideal of poverty in a more literal sense. Not unlike Paul in 1 Corinthians 7, Catherine recommends this latter calling as preferable or more "perfect," while making room for the other more general calling as a faithful expression of Christian practice. By doing this, she is able to engage in extreme actions herself on behalf of the poor while not making a legalistic declaration that all Christians must live in exactly the same manner.

While it may sound strange or offensive to hear what sounds like Catherine glorifying poverty, we should not interpret her as saying it is good not to have enough to live on. She took a vow to pursue poverty as part of her religious vocation. At the same time, as with the other writers we have read, Catherine maintains that Christian mission can never be divorced from action on behalf of and alongside the poor. This reading begins as God's words to Catherine and ends as her prayer to God.

Text

The Dialogue

1. . . . Those who would possess the gold of this world's goods acquire and possess it by the light of reason. But those who would go the way of great perfection spurn that gold in actuality as well as in spirit. These follow both materially and in spirit the counsel given and bequeathed by my Truth, while those with possessions keep the commandments, but observe the counsels in spirit only.

However, since the counsels are bound up with the commandments, no one can keep the commandments without following the counsels at least in spirit if not materially. Though they may possess the riches of the world, they must own them humbly, not with pride, as things lent to them rather as their own—for in my generosity I give you these things for your use. You have as much as I give you: you keep as much as I allow you to keep; and I give and let you keep as much as I see would be good for you.

This is the spirit in which people should use things, and if they do, they will be keeping the command that you love me above all things and your neighbor as your very self. They will live with their heart emptied of material things, cutting them off from their affection. In other words, they will neither love nor possess them apart from my will. Though they may in fact have possessions, they will be following the counsel in spirit by cutting off from themselves the venomous sting of disordered love. This is the way of ordinary love.

But those who keep the commandments and counsels actually as well as in spirit go the way of perfect love. They follow in true simplicity the counsel my Truth, the incarnate Word, gave to that young man when he asked, "What can I do, Master, to win eternal life?" He said, "Keep the commandments of the Law." The other answered, "I do keep them." And he said, "Well, if you want to be perfect go and sell what you have and give to the poor."

Then the young man was sad. He was still too much in love with what wealth he had, and that is why he was sad. But those who are perfect heed what he said. They let go of the world and all its pleasures. They discipline their bodies with penance and vigils, with constant humble prayer.

Those, however, who go the way of ordinary love without actually rising above material things (for they are not obliged to do so) do not thereby forfeit eternal life. But if they wish to have this world's goods they must possess them in the way I told you. To have these things is not sinful. After all, everything is good and perfect, created

by me, Goodness itself. But I made these things to serve
my rational creatures; I did not intend my creatures to make
themselves servants and slave to the world's pleasures.
So if they would not go the way of great perfection, they
may keep these things if they choose, but they will be
servants, less than lords. They owe their first love to me.
Everything else they should love and possess, as I told
you, not as if they owned it but as something lent them.

I am not a respecter of person or status but of holy desires.
In whatever situation people may be, let their will be good
and holy, and they will be pleasing to me.

Who are they who possess this world's goods in this
way? Those who have cut the venomous sting off them
by despising their selfish sensuality and loving virtue.
Once they have cut off the venom of disorder from their
will and set it in order with love and holy fear of me,
they can choose and hold whatever situation they will
and still be fit to have eternal life. It remains true that
it is more perfect and more pleasing to me to rise above
all the world's goods in fact as well as in spirit. But those
who feel that their weakness will not let them reach such
perfection can travel this ordinary way according to their
own situation. My goodness has ordained it thus, so that
no one in any situation whatever should have an excuse
for sin.

Indeed they have no excuse. For I have made allowance
for their passions and weaknesses in such a way that if
they choose to remain in the world they can. They can
possess wealth and hold positions of authority. They can
be married and care for their children and toil for them.
They can remain in any situation whatever, so long as

they truly cut off the venomous sting of selfish sensuality that deals eternal death.

And it surely is venomous. For just as venom is painful to the body and ultimately cases death unless a person makes the effort to vomit it out and take some medicine, so it is with this scorpion of the world's pleasure. I am not speaking of material things in themselves. I have already told you that these are good and that they are made by me, the greatest Good, and so you can use them as you please with holy love and truthful fear. What I am speaking of is the venom of a perverted human will, which poisons souls and causes them death, unless they vomit it up through a holy confession, tearing their heart and affection free from it. Such confession is a medicine that heals the effects of this venom even while it tastes bitter to selfish sensuality . . .

2. Now I want to tell you just a little bit about the ways I have to help my servants who trust in me in their bodily needs. I provide for all of them, but they receive my help perfectly or imperfectly according to how perfect or imperfect, how detached from the world and themselves, they are. Take for example my poor—those who are poor in spirit and in will, that is in spiritual intent. I do not simply say "poor," because there are many who are poor but would rather not be. These are rich so far as their will is concerned, and beggars insofar as they neither trust in me nor willingly bear the poverty I have given them as medicine for their souls because wealth would have been bad for them and would have been their damnation.

My servants, on the other hand, are poor but not beggars. Beggars often do not have what they need and suffer great want. But the poor, thought they do not enjoy plenty, have their every need fulfilled; I never fail them so long as they put their trust in me. True, I sometimes bring them to the brink so that they will better see and know that I can and will provide for them, so that they will fall in love with my providence and embrace true poverty as their bride. Then their servant, the Holy Spirit, my mercy, when he sees that they lack anything that is necessary for their bodies, will light a nudging spark of desire in the hearts of those who are able to help, and these will come to help them in their need. The whole life of my gentle poor is thus cared for by the concern I give the world's servants for them. While it is true that in order to prove their patience and faith and perseverance I allow them to suffer reproach and insult and abuse, at the same time my mercy constrains the very persons who treat them ill to give them alms and help them in their need. Such is my general providence for my poor.

But sometimes, for my great servants, I act directly, by myself alone, without any human intermediary, as you know from your own experience. And you have heard how your glorious father Dominic, in the early days of the Order, was once so in need that when it came time to eat, the brothers had nothing. My beloved servant Dominic, trusting by the light of faith that I would provide, said, "Sons, take your places at table." They brothers obeyed him, and at his word sat down. Then I who provide for those who trust in me sent two angels with the whitest of bread, so much that they had great plenty for several meals. This was an instance of providence worked by the Holy Spirit's mercy without any human intermediary.

Sometimes I provide by multiplying a little bit of something that would never have been enough, as you know I did for that gentle virgin Saint Agnes.[3] From her childhood right up to the end she served me with true humility and such firm trust that she never had any hesitations concerning herself or her family. So with her lively faith, at the command of Mary this poor young thing without any temporal goods began to establish a monastery. You know that the place had been a brothel. She didn't think, "How will I be able to do this?" But with my providence she quickly made it a holy place, a monastery for religious . . . Among other things, I once let them go three days without bread, with nothing but greens to eat. You might ask me, "Why did you do this in spite of the fact that you told me that you never fail your servants who trust in you and that they always have what they need? It seems to me that these women did not have what they needed, because the human body cannot live on nothing but greens . . . " I would answer you that I did it and permitted it to make Agnes drunk with my providence . . .

I told you I provide by multiplying things. At the time I was telling you about, Agnes turned her mind's eye to me in the light of faith and said, "My Father and Lord, my eternal bridegroom, did you make me take these daughters away from their fathers' homes to die of hunger? Provide, Lord, for their need." It was I who made her ask. I was pleased to test her faith, and her humble prayer was pleasing to me. I stretched out my providence to a certain person who was standing in spirit before me, and I constrained him by my inspiration to bring them five little rolls. I revealed this to Agnes' mind, and she

---

3   Anges Segni of Montepulciano, not Agnes of Prague.

turned to her sisters and said, "Go to the turn, my daughters, and bring that bread." When they had brought it back they took their places at table. I gave her such power as she divided up the bread that all of them ate their fill and so much was left on the table that they had plenty for their bodily need yet another time.

This is the providence I use with my servants who are poor by choice, and not simply by choice but for spiritual reasons. For without their spiritual intention it would be worthless. They would be like the philosophers who for love of science and their will to learn it spurned riches and became poor by choice because they knew naturally that worrying about worldly riches would prevent their reaching the scientific goal they had set before their mind's eye as their sole end. But because their choice of poverty was not spiritual, not made for the glory and praise of my name, it did not bring them grace or perfection but eternal death.

3. But alas, dearest daughter, see how those philosophers put to shame the miserable lovers of wealth who do not follow the knowledge offered them by nature to gain the supreme eternal Good! For the philosophers, knowing wealth was a hindrance to them, threw it off. But these people would make wealth a god. It is clear that this is so from the fact that they grieve more when they lose their wealth and temporal possessions than when they lose me, the supreme eternal wealth.

If you will look well, you will see that every sort of evil comes from this perverse desire and will for wealth. Pride comes from it, because they want to be superior. It brings forth injustice to themselves and to others. It brings forth [greed], because their hunger for money makes them think nothing of robbing their brothers [and sisters] or taking what belongs to the Church, what has been bought with the blood of the Word, my only-begotten Son. It generates trafficking in the flesh of their neighbors and selling time as usurers who like thieves sell what is not theirs to sell. It generates gluttony for too much and too many foods. And indecency, for if they had nothing to spend they would not be keeping company with such wretchedness.

How many murders! How much hatred and spite toward their neighbors! What cruelty and unfaithfulness to me, because they presume on themselves as if they had acquired their wealth by their own power! They do not see that they neither gain nor keep it by their own power but only by mine. They lose their trust in me and trust only in their riches. But their trust is empty, for it will fail as soon as they have no more riches. Either they will lose them in this life by my dispensation and for their own good, or they will lose them in death. Then they will know how fickle and empty their trust was. It impoverishes and kills the soul. It makes people cruel to themselves. It takes away the worth of the infinite and makes it finite; that is, their desire, which ought to be united with me, infinite Good, is united with and set on the love of something finite. They lose their taste for virtue and for the fragrance of poverty, they lose their lordship by becoming the servants of riches. They are never satisfied, because they love something that is less than themselves. All created things were made to serve people, not for people to become their servants, and people ought to be serving me, for I am their end.

To what dangers and sufferings people will submit
themselves on land and sea to acquire great wealth,
to return to their own city with pleasures and honors!
Yet they neither try nor care to acquire the virtues or to
suffer the least bit of pain to have them, though these are
the riches of the soul. They are totally immersed [in their
wealth], and their heart and affection, which ought to
be serving me, they have set on wealth, loading their
conscience with all sorts of unlawful gains. See to what
wretchedness they have come, what it is they serve:
not firm and stable things but changeable things, so that
today they are rich, tomorrow poor. Now they are high
up, now low. Now they are feared and respected by the
world because of their wealth, and now they are ridiculed
for having lost it. They are treated with reproach and
shame and no compassion, because they were loved and
made themselves loved for their riches and not for their
virtue. If they had made themselves loved and been loved
for their virtue, they would have lost neither respect nor
love, because they would have lost only their temporal
possessions but not the riches of virtue.

Oh, what a heavy weight these are to their conscience!
They are so heavy that they can neither run along this road
of pilgrimage nor pass through the narrow gate. Thus my
Truth said in the holy Gospel that it is more impossible for
a rich person to enter eternal life than for a camel to pass
through the eye of a needle . . . They cannot pass through
the gate because it is narrow and low. Only if they throw
their load to the ground and restrain their affection for the
world and bow their head in humility will they be able
to pass through. And there is no other gate but this that
leads to eternal life.

The gate is broad that leads to eternal damnation, and blind as they are it seems they do not see their own destruction, for even in this life they have a foretaste of hell. They are always suffering because they are wanting more than they can have. They suffer over what they do not have, and what they lose they lose with grief. Their grief is as great as was their love in possessing. They lose all affection for their neighbors and have no care for acquiring virtue.

O rottenness of the world! Not the things of the world in themselves, because I created everything good and perfect. But rotten are those who seek and keep these things with disordered love.

Dearest daughter, your tongue could never tell how many are the evils that come from this. They see and experience them every day, but they do not want to see or recognize their harmfulness.

4. I have touched on these few things because I want you to know better the treasure of spiritually motivated voluntary poverty. Who knows it? My beloved poor servants who in order to be able to travel this road and enter through this narrow gate have thrown to the ground the burden of riches.

Some throw it down both in fact and in spirit: These are those who observe both the commandments and the counsel in fact as well as in spirit. The others observe the counsel in spirit only, stripping themselves of attachment to wealth, so that they do not possess it with disordered love but with holy fear. In fact, they are not so much possessors of it as distributors for the poor. This is good, but the first way is perfect, more fruitful and less

encumbered, and there my providence is more clearly
reflected in actuality . . . Both the one and the other bow
their heads, making themselves small in true humility.
But because I have told you elsewhere about the second—
if you remember well, I did tell you something about
it—I will now tell you only about the first.

I have shown you how every evil, harm, and suffering, in
this life and in the next, comes from selfish love of riches.

Now, on the opposite side, I am telling you that every
good, peace, rest, and calm comes from poverty. Only look
at the faces of those who are truly poor: how happy and
joyful they are! The only thing that saddens them is when
I am offended, and this sadness fattens rather than
distresses the soul. Through poverty they have gained
the highest of riches. By leaving darkness behind they
discover the most perfect light for themselves. By leaving
behind worldly sadness they have come to possess
happiness. In place of mortal goods they find the immortal.
The greatest of consolations is theirs. Their labors and
suffering are refreshment to them. They are just and love
everyone with a familial love. They do not play favorites.

In whom do the virtues of most holy faith and true hope
shine forth? Where does the fire of divine charity burn?
In those who, by the light of their faith in me, supreme
eternal wealth, raise their hope above the world and above
all empty riches to embrace true poverty as their bride . . .
With this faith and hope, ablaze with the fire of charity,
my true servants leaped and leap above riches and
selfishness. Just so, the glorious apostle Matthew leaped
up from his tax booth and, leaving his great wealth
behind, followed my Truth, who taught you the way and

the rule by teaching you to love and follow this poverty. And he taught you not only with words but by his example as well, from his birth right up to the end of his life. For you he took poverty as his bride, though he was wealth itself by his union with the divine nature, for he is one thing with me and I with him, eternal wealth.

And if you would see him humiliated and in great poverty, look at God made man, clothed in the lowliness of your humanity.

You see this gentle loving Word born in a stable while Mary was on a journey, to show you pilgrims how you should be constantly born anew in the stable of self-knowledge, where by grace you will find me born within your soul. You see him lying there among the animals, in such poverty that Mary had nothing to cover him up with. It was winter, and she kept him warm with the animals' breath and a blanket of hay. He is the fire of charity but he chose to endure the cold in his humanity.

All the while he lived he chose to suffer, whether his disciples joined him or not, as when once because of their hunger the disciples plucked ears of corn and ate the grain.

At the end of his life, stripped naked, scourged at the pillar, parched with thirst, he was so poor on the wood of the cross that neither the earth nor the wood could give him a place to lay his head. He had nowhere to rest it except on his own shoulder. And drunk as he was with love, he made a bath for you of his blood when this Lamb's body was broken open and bled from every part.

Out of his misery he gave you great wealth. From the narrow wood of the cross he extended his generosity to everyone. By tasting the bitterness of the gall he gave you the most perfect sweetness. From his sadness he gave you consolation. He was nailed to the cross to loose you from the chains of deadly sin. By becoming a servant he rescued you from slavery to the devil and set you free. He was sold to ransom you with his blood. By choosing death for himself he gave you life.

"Out of his misery he gave you great wealth."

How truly, then, has he given you love as your rule by showing you more love than you could ever show, giving his life for you who were enemies to him and to me the high eternal Father . . . He gave you true humility as your rule by humbling himself in his shameful death on the cross. He gave you lowliness as your rule by suffering such disgrace and great reproach. And he gave you true poverty as your rule, for Scripture laments in his name, "The foxes have dens, the birds have nests, but the Virgin's Son has nowhere to lay his head." Who knows this? Those who are enlightened by most holy faith. In whom do you find this faith? In the spiritually poor who have taken as their bride Queen Poverty, for they have cast away the riches that bring on the darkness of infidelity.

This queen's realm is never at war, but is always peaceful and calm. She overflows with justice, because the thing that perpetrates injustice is cut off from her. Her city walls are strong, because their foundation is not in the earth, nor on the sand that every little wind scares up from the earth, but on the living rock, the gentle Christ Jesus my only-begotten Son. There is no darkness within her, but fire without any cold, because this queen's mother is divine charity. This city's adornment is compassion and mercy, because the cruel tyrant wealth has been put out. There is benevolence, that is, neighborly affection, among all its citizens. There is enduring perseverance and prudence, for poverty does not act or govern her city imprudently but watches over it with great concern and prudence. Thus the soul who take this gentle queen, poverty, as bride is made master of all these riches, for the two go hand in hand.

The soul who takes Queen Poverty as bride . . . has no fear of vexation, for no one is at war with her. She has no fear of hunger or want, because her faith sees and trusts me, her Creator and the source of all wealth and providence, for I always feed and nurture her. Have you ever found a servant of mine, a spouse of poverty, who died of hunger? No. There have been some who had great and overflowing riches and have perished because they trusted in their riches rather than in me. But I never fail those who never fail in their hope. I provide for them as a kind compassionate father . . . True, I let them suffer to make them grow in faith and hope and so that I may reward them for their labors, but I never fail to give them anything they need . . . They are people in love and alive in my will, ready to endure heat, cold, and nakedness, hunger and thirst, anguish and abuse and even death, in their desire to give their life for love of Life (that is, for me, for I am their life).

Look at the poor apostles and the other glorious martyrs, Peter, Paul, and Stephen. Look at Lawrence, who seems to be not over the fire but over the most pleasant of flowers, joking, as it were, with the tyrant and saying, "This side is cooked; turn it over and start eating!" The fire of divine charity was so great that in his soul's feeling he regarded the lesser fire as nothing . . . These souls became obedient both in fact and in spirit to the commandments and to the counsels given them by my Truth.

Who would not have judged that poor Lazarus was supremely miserable and the rich man quite happy and content? Yet such was not the case, for that rich man with all his wealth suffered more than poor Lazarus tormented by his leprosy. For the rich man's [selfish] will was alive, and this is the source of all suffering. But in Lazarus this will was dead and his will was so alive in me that he found refreshment and consolation in his pain. He had been thrown out by others, especially by the rich man, and was neither cleansed nor cared for by them, but I provided that the senseless animals should lick his sores. And you see how at the end of their lives Lazarus has eternal life and the rich man is in hell.

So the rich are left sad while my poor are happy. I hold them to my breast and give them the milk of great consolation. Because they leave everything they possess me completely. The Holy Spirit becomes the nurse of their souls and their little bodies in every situation. I make the animals provide for them in this way and that, depending on their need. If a hermit is ill I make another hermit leave his cell to help him . . . In every way I provide for [my poor].

So you see, most beloved daughter, how great is the contentment and delight of these beloved poor of mine.

5. Then that soul was as if drunk with love of true holy poverty. She was filled to bursting in the supreme eternal magnificence and so transformed in the abyss of his supreme and immeasurable providence that though she was in the vessel of her body it seemed as if the fire of charity within her had taken over and rapt[4] her outside her body. And with her mind's eye steadily fixed on the divine majesty she spoke to the high eternal Father:

O eternal Father! O fiery abyss of charity! O eternal beauty, O eternal wisdom, O eternal goodness, O eternal mercy! O hope and refuge of sinners! O immeasurable generosity! O eternal, infinite Good! O mad lover! And you have need of your creature? It seems to me, for you act as if you could not live without her, in spite of the fact that you are Life itself, and everything has life from you and nothing can have life without you. Why then are you so mad? Because you have fallen in love with what you have made! You are pleased and delighted over her within yourself, as if you were drunk [with desire] for her

---

4　Rapt – carried away or transported

salvation. She runs away from you and you go looking for her. She strays and you draw closer to her. You clothed yourself in our humanity, and nearer than that you could not have come.

And what shall I say? I will stutter, "A-a," because there is nothing else I know how to say . . .

Discussion Questions

 How does Catherine connect the desire for wealth to systems of injustice and violence? How is your community shaped by people pursuing wealth? How does it affect those who are poor?

 Catherine makes an important distinction between commandment and counsel. How does she understand the difference between the two? How could this distinction help you think about different callings in regard to wealth and poverty?

 Clare praises poverty and Catherine calls poverty a Queen. Why would they feel this way about poverty? What is your heart's desire?

 Clare grew up in wealth and chose to leave it behind. She praises the ruler Agnes for using her wealth and position in service to the poor. How might God want to use your hands? Are there things he is calling you leave behind? To give away? To use, like Agnes, for the pursuit of justice?

 Catherine prays to be consumed by God, whom she describes as a fiery abyss of charity and as drunk with desire for her. Are there practices of prayer and meditation that would help guide you in regard to money, charity, and justice?

Chapter 5

Church Teaching

In cases of need all things are common property, so
that there would seem to be no sin in taking another's
property, for need has made it common.

~ Thomas Aquinas

THOMAS AQUINAS (1225–1274)

Background

Thomas Aquinas is celebrated as one of the greatest
systematic theologians of the church. In his enormous
work the *Summa Theologica*, he strives to present the
orthodox consensus of church teaching down through
the ages. His work is far-ranging and addresses all manner
of issues, including economics and ethics. Among many
other things, he demonstrates how the Western church of
the Middle Ages tended to think about money and poverty.

The work of Aquinas has been influential in the development of modern ideas about law and economics. He is a proponent of natural theology, the idea that God is known through nature and the natural order of things as well as in Scripture and church teaching.

Aquinas' work has come to represent the intellectual fervor of reasoned church teaching. At the same time, Aquinas himself was given to miraculous visions of Christ's glory and eventually stopped writing the *Summa*, saying that all he had written seemed to him like "straw" compared to his experience of the living Jesus. This doesn't mean that he rejected his work but that he saw it as paling in comparison to his experience of God.

Aquinas is important to include among the other writers because he shows that, even if one does not embrace the radical poverty of the Franciscans, Christian teaching throughout the ages does not support an inordinate or unjust accumulation of wealth (of course, Christian teaching and Christian practice have not always been the same in this regard). As a medieval theologian, Aquinas used a style of writing that asks questions and then answers them. Aquinas normally presents a few objections to his teaching, then summarizes his main point, and finally replies to the objections one by one. Since this style of writing may be unfamiliar to modern readers, I have reordered it so that we first hear Aquinas' main point and then hear him present objections and replies together. In the brief and edited examples that follow, Aquinas tackles five questions: Is it okay to have private property? Is it wrong to steal? Is it wrong to take someone else's property if you are in need? Is it wrong to charge usury (interest on loans for the daily necessities of life)? Is it wrong to take out a loan at interest to pay for one's needs?

As Aquinas thinks through how Christian mission relates to poverty, we will hear him quote Basil and some of the other authors we have already read.

Text

Summa Theologica, Section 3, Question 66

1.   It is lawful for a man to possess a thing as his own? (§2)

I answer that, Two things are acceptable for man in relation to exterior things. One is the power to obtain them and distribute them, and in this regard it is lawful for man to possess property. In addition, this is necessary to human life for three reasons. First because every man is more careful to obtain what is for himself alone than that which is common to many or to all: since each one would neglect the labor and leave to another that which concerns the community, as happens where there is a great number of servants. Secondly, because human affairs are conducted in more orderly fashion if each man is charged with taking care of some particular thing himself, whereas there would be confusion if everyone had to look after any one thing indeterminately. Thirdly, because a more peaceful state is ensured to man if each one is content with his own. In this way, it is should be seen that quarrels arise more frequently where there is no division of the things possessed.

The second thing that is acceptable to man with regard to external things is their use. On this respect man ought to possess external things, not as his own, but as common, so that, to say, he is ready to communicate them to others in their need. In this way, the Apostle says (1 Tim 6:17–18): "Charge the rich of this world . . . to give easily, to communicate to others," etc.

Objection 2 [against Aquinas]. . . . Basil in expounding the words of the rich man quoted above (Article 1, Objection 2), says: "The rich who call their own property the common goods they have seized upon, are like those who go to the play beforehand and then prevent others from coming, and take for themselves what is intended for common use." Now it would be unlawful to prevent others from obtaining possession of common goods. Therefore it is unlawful to take for oneself what belongs to the community.

Reply to Objection 2 [Aquinas' reply]. A man would not act unlawfully if by going to the play beforehand he prepared the way for others: but he acts unlawfully if by so doing he keeps others from going. In a similar way a rich man does not act unlawfully if he looks after someone by taking possession of something which at first was common property, and gives others a share: but he sins if he excludes others indiscriminately from using it. Hence Basil says (Hom. in Luc. xii, 18): "Why are you rich while another is poor, unless it is so that you may have the merit of good stewardship, and he the reward of patience?"

2. Is theft always a sin? (§5)

It is written (Exod 20:15): "You shall not steal."

I answer that, If anyone consider what is meant by theft, he will find that it is sinful on two counts. First, because of its opposition to justice, which gives to each one what is his, so that for this reason theft is contrary to justice, because it involves taking what belongs to another.

Secondly, because of the guile or fraud committed by the thief, by laying hands on another's property secretly and cunningly. This is why it is clear that every theft is a sin.

3. Is it lawful to steal because of stress of need? (§7)

In cases of need all things are common property, so that there would seem to be no sin in taking another's property, for need has made it common.

I answer that, Things which are of human right cannot detract from natural right or Divine right. Now according to the natural order established by Divine Providence, inferior things are ordained for the purpose of taking care of man's needs by their means. This is why the division and appropriation of things which are based on human law, do not prevent the fact that man's needs have to be taken care of by means of these very things. Therefore whatever certain people have in superabundance is due, by natural law, to the purpose of taking care of the poor. For this reason Ambrose [Loc. cit., Article 2, Objection 3] says, and his words are embodied in the Decretals (Dist. xlvii, can. Sicut ii): "It is the hungry man's bread that you withhold, the naked man's cloak that you store away, the money that you bury in the earth is the price of the poor man's ransom and freedom."

Since, however, there are many who are in need, while it is impossible for all to be taken care of by means of the same thing, each one is entrusted with the stewardship of his own things, so that out of them he may come to the aid of those who are in need. Nevertheless, if the need is so manifest and urgent, that it is evident that the present need must be taken care of by whatever means be at hand (for instance when a person is in some imminent danger, and there is no other possible remedy), then it is lawful for a man to take care of his own need by means of another's property, by taking it either openly or secretly: this is not properly speaking theft or robbery.

Summa Theologica, Section 3, Question 78

4. *Whether it is a sin to take usury¹ for money lent? (§1)*

It is written (Exod 22:25): "If you lend money to any of your people that is poor, that dwells with you, you shall not be hard upon them as an extortioner, nor oppress them with usuries."

I answer that, To take usury for money lent is unjust in itself, because this is to sell what does not exist, and this evidently leads to inequality which is contrary to justice. In order to make this evident, we must observe that there are certain things which exist to be used by being consumed: thus we consume wine when we use it for drink and we consume wheat when we use it for food. This is why in such like things the use of the thing must not be calculated apart from the thing itself, and whoever is granted the use of the thing, is granted the thing itself and for this reason, to lend things of this kind is to transfer the ownership. Accordingly if a man wanted to sell wine separately from the use of the wine, he would be selling the same thing twice, or he would be selling what does not exist, which is why he would evidently commit a sin of injustice. On like manner he commits an injustice who lends wine or wheat, and asks for double payment, (in other words, one, the return of the thing in

---

1   Usury – to loan at interest, usually at unreasonably high rates or for the purchase of necessities or things that are consumed.

equal measure, the other, the price of the use, which is called usury).

On the other hand, there are things which do not exist simply to be consumed: thus to use a house is to dwell in it, not to destroy it. This is why in such things both may be granted: for instance, one man may hand over to another the ownership of his house while reserving to himself the use of it for a time, or vice versa, he may grant the use of the house, while retaining the ownership. For this reason a man may lawfully make a charge for the use of his house, and, besides this, reclaim the house from the person to whom he has granted its use, as happens in renting and leasing a house.

Now money, according to the Philosopher[2] (Ethic. v, 5; Polit. i, 3) was invented chiefly for the purpose of exchange: and consequently the proper and principal use of money is its consumption or transfer whereby it is sunk in exchange. Therefore it is by its very nature unlawful to take payment for the use of money lent, which payment is known as usury: and just as a man is bound to restore other ill-gotten goods, so is he bound to restore the money which he has taken in usury.

Objection 2 [against Aquinas]. Further, according to Psalm 18:8, "The law of the Lord is unspotted," because, to say, it forbids sin. Now a type of usury is allowed in the Divine law, according to Deuteronomy 23:19–20: "You shall not fenerate[3] to your brother money, nor corn, nor any other thing, but to the stranger": yet even more, it is even promised as a reward for the observance of the Law,

---

2 Philosopher – a reference to Aristotle.

3 Fenerate – to engage in usury, to loan at interest.

according to Deuteronomy 28:12: "You shall fenerate to many nations, and shall not borrow of any one." . . . Therefore it is not a sin to take usury.

Reply to Objection 2 [Aquinas' reply]. The Jews were forbidden to take usury from their brethren, i.e. from other Jews. By this we are given to understand that to take usury from any man is evil simply, because we ought to treat every man as our neighbor and brother, especially in the state of the Gospel, to which all are called. Therefore it is said without any distinction in Psalm 14:5: "He that has not put out his money to usury," and (Ezek 18:8): "Who has not taken usury [Vulgate: 'If a man . . . has not lent upon money, nor taken any increase . . . he is just.']." They were permitted, however, to take usury from foreigners, not as though it were lawful, but in order to avoid a greater evil, lest, to say, through the greed to which they were prone according to Isaiah 56:11, they should take usury from the Jews who were worshippers of God.

Where we find it promised to them as a reward, "You shall fenerate to many nations," etc., fenerating is to be taken in a broad sense for lending, as in Sirach 29:10, where we read: "Many have refused to fenerate, not out of wickedness," i.e. they would not lend. Accordingly the Jews are promised in reward an abundance of wealth, so that they would be able to lend to others.

Objection 3 [against Aquinas]. Further, in human affairs justice is determined by civil laws. Now civil law allows usury to be taken. Therefore it seems to be lawful.

Reply to Objection 3 [Aquinas' reply]. Human laws leave certain things unpunished, because of the condition of those who are imperfect, and who would be deprived of many advantages, if all sins were strictly forbidden and punishments appointed for them. This is why human law has permitted usury, not that it looks upon usury as harmonizing with justice, but so that the advantage of many should not be hindered. Therefore in civil law [Inst. II, iv, *de Usufructu*] it is stated that "those things according to natural reason and civil law which are consumed by being used, do not allow usury," and that "the senate did not (nor could it) appoint a usury to such things, but established a quasi-usury," namely by permitting usury. Moreover the Philosopher, led by natural reason, says (Polit. i, 3) that "to make money by usury is exceedingly unnatural."

Objection 5 [against Aquinas]. Further, it does not seem to be in itself sinful to accept a price for doing what one is not required to do. But one who has money is not required in every case to lend it to his neighbor. Therefore it is lawful for him sometimes to accept a price for lending it.

Reply to Objection 5 [Aquinas' reply]. He that is not required to lend, may accept repayment for what he has done, but he must not charge more. Now he is repaid according to equality of justice if he is repaid as much as he lent. This is why if he charges more for the use of a thing which has no other use but the consumption of its substance, he charges a price of something that does not exist: and so his charge is unjust.

Objection 7 [against Aquinas]. Further, anyone may lawfully accept a thing which its owner freely gives him. Now he who accepts the loan, freely gives the usury. Therefore he who lends may lawfully take the usury.

Reply to Objection 7 [Aquinas' reply]. He who gives usury does not give it voluntarily simply, but under a certain necessity, in so far as he needs to borrow money which the owner is unwilling to lend without usury.

5. Is it lawful to borrow money under a condition of usury? (§4)

He that suffers injury does not sin, according to the Philosopher (Ethic. v, 11), this is why justice is not a middle ground between two vices, as is stated in the same book (ch. 5). Now a usurer sins by doing an injury to the person who borrows from him under a condition of usury. Therefore he that accepts a loan under a condition of usury does not sin.

I answer that, It is by no means lawful to induce a man to sin, yet it is lawful to make use of another's sin for a good end, since even God uses all sin for some good, since He draws some good from every evil as stated in the Enchiridion (xi). Hence when Publicola asked whether it were lawful to make use of an oath taken by a man swearing by false gods (which is a manifest sin, for he gives Divine honor to them) Augustine (Ep. xlvii) answered that he who uses, not for a bad but for a good purpose, the oath of a man that swears by false gods, is a party, not to his sin of swearing by demons, but to his good contract by which he kept his word. If however he were to persuade him to swear by false gods, he would sin.

Accordingly we must also answer to the question in point that it is by no means lawful to persuade a man to lend under a condition of usury: yet it is lawful to borrow for

usury from a man who is ready to do so and is a usurer
by profession; provided the borrower have a good end in
view, such as the relief of his own or another's need. Thus
too it is lawful for a man who has fallen among thieves to
point out his property to them (which they sin in taking)
in order to save his life, after the example of the ten men
who said to Ishmael (Jer 41:8): "Kill us not: for we have
stores in the field."

Objection 1 [against Aquinas]. It would seem that it is not
lawful to borrow money under a condition of usury. For the
Apostle says (Rom 1:32) that they "are worthy of death . . .
not only they that do" these sins, "but they also that consent
to them that do them." Now he that borrows money under
a condition of usury consents in the sin of the usurer, and
gives him an occasion of sin. Therefore he sins also.

Reply to Objection 1 [Aquinas' reply]. He who borrows for
usury does not consent to the usurer's sin but makes use
of it. Nor is it the usurer's acceptance of usury that pleases
him, but his lending, which is good.

Objection 2 [against Aquinas]. Further, no one should, for
temporal advantage, give another an occasion of committing
a sin: for this pertains to active scandal, which is always
sinful, as stated above (II–II:43:2). Now he that seeks to
borrow from a usurer gives him an occasion of sin.
Therefore he is not to be excused on account of any
temporal advantage.

Reply to Objection 2 [Aquinas' reply]. He who borrows for
usury gives the usurer an occasion, not for taking usury,
but for lending; it is the usurer who finds an occasion of
sin in the malice of his heart. Therefore there is passive

scandal on his part, while there is no active scandal on the part of the person who seeks to borrow. Nor is this passive scandal a reason why the other person should abstain from borrowing if he is in need, since this passive scandal arises not from weakness or ignorance but from malice.

Discussion Questions

Aquinas says that stealing in times of extreme need is not theft. What would he say about those who prevent others from accessing the basic necessities of life? Does this happen in your community?

Why does Aquinas say private ownership is a good thing? How does his view of private ownership differ from the modern "free market"?

In Genesis 2, God gave all the trees in the garden to humanity in general (plural "you"). How might Aquinas be applying this passage? How does this understanding of God caring for all humanity affect your feelings toward others?

Why would Aquinas say that charging usury is a sin while accepting loans with usury is not? Why would he defend the victims of usury but not its perpetrators? Is the way you are using your hands helping or hurting yourself and others?

How does Aquinas's critique of usury relate to today? How should we live in regard to practices like holding mortgages and land contracts, charging others interest, applying for payday loans, purchasing on a rent-to-own basis, and taking on or accumulating debt? What habits should those with financial means develop in regard to using money justly?

GLOBAL MISSION

Chapter 6

A Protestant Response

And so we find that all our labor is nothing more than the finding and collecting of God's gifts; it is quite unable to create or preserve anything.

~ Martin Luther

MARTIN LUTHER (1483–1546)

Background

Martin Luther was a German Augustinian monk who spearheaded the Protestant Reformation. In 1518, as he was reading the first chapter of Paul's letter to the Romans and meditating on God's righteousness being revealed through faith, he experienced what he described as a conversion. From then on, he became a committed proponent of the view that salvation is by grace alone through faith and not by works. He became a fierce critic of any church practice that smacked of works-righteousness or salvation by anything other than grace. He translated the Bible into German so that the common person could read it. With the use of the new technology made available in Gutenberg's printing press, the Scriptures and Luther's writings could be transmitted widely. He was a vocal opponent of the pope and anyone in power whom he saw as taking advantage of others spiritually or economically.

At the famous Diet of Worms (a hearing before the political/religious powers), Luther was asked to recant his writings. After carefully considering his course of action, he replied that he would be willing to take back some of his more confrontational writings but that he could not recant his belief in salvation by grace through faith. He maintained that his conscience was captive to the Word of God. He is traditionally held to have answered, "Here I stand, I can do no other. God help me." Luther was subsequently excommunicated, unable to take part in communion as a member of the Roman Catholic Church.

Luther had a personality larger than life. While he shared all the foibles[1] common to humanity, he has profoundly shaped Christian experience throughout the centuries. Some of his last words are held to have been, "We are beggars; that is the truth." In the following reading, Luther writes with his characteristic plain language and his insightful biblical exegesis. He offers a profound theological reading of Psalm 127 for the average Christian. In it, he masterfully weaves together notions about the provision of God and the role of humans. While in other writings Luther argues

---

1 Foible – a minor weakness

against usury and many unjust business practices of his day, in this writing Luther considers questions related to money, wealth, poverty, and Christian mission.

Text

Exposition of Psalm 127, For the Christians at Riga in Livonia

Martin Luther to all his dear friends in Christ at Riga and in Livonia.

Grace and peace from God our Father through our Lord Jesus Christ . . .

I selected this psalm because it so beautifully turns the heart away from covetousness and concern for temporal livelihood and possessions toward faith in God, and in a few words teaches us how Christians are to act with respect to the accumulation and ownership of this world's goods. It is hardly to be expected that the gospel, which has now again come to the fore, will fare any better among us and among you than it did at the time of Christ and the apostles, indeed, since the beginning of the world. For not only the evangelists, but all the prophets as well, complain that covetousness and concern for this world's goods hinder the gospel greatly from bearing fruit. Indeed, the precious word of God sometimes falls among thorns and is choked (Matt 13:22) so that it proves unfruitful; sadly enough, our daily experience shows us this only too well. And Paul also complains that all seek their own interests, not those of Jesus Christ (Phil 2:21).

Now I have preached and written a great deal urging that good schools should be established in the cities in order

that we might produce educated men and women, whence
good Christian pastors and preachers might come forth
so that the word of God might continue to flourish richly.
But people take such an indifferent attitude toward the
matter, pretending that it might cost them their whole
livelihood and temporal possessions, that I fear the time
will come when schoolmasters, pastors, and preachers
alike will have to quit, let the word go, and turn to a trade
or some other means of stilling the pangs of hunger; just
as the Levites had to abandon the worship of God to till
the fields, as Nehemiah writes (Neh 13:10) . . .

Now that God is sending us upright, trustworthy, and
learned men, who by word and deed encourage us toward
self-discipline and chastity, who by godly marriage reduce
the prevalence of fornication, and who in addition zealously
serve us in body and soul and direct us on the right path
to heaven, we simply ignore them. Those whom we should
be securing at whatever expense even from the ends of
the earth, we are supporting about as well as the rich man
supported poor Lazarus (Luke 16:19–21) . . .

For this reason I want yet to sing one little song for the
benefit of such covetousness, that some might still be roused
to help us ward off the wrath of God a bit longer . . .

Solomon composed this psalm. Not only was he
enlightened by the Holy Spirit, but as he daily exercised
his administrative functions and mingled with people,
he learned from frequent experience how vainly unbelief
burdens itself with worries about feeding the belly,
when in fact everything depends on God's blessing and
protection. For where God withholds his blessing, we

labor in vain; where God does not protect, our worry is futile. And he speaks thus:

1a. Unless the Lord builds the house,
those who build it labor in vain.

1b. Unless the Lord watches over the city,
the watchman stays awake in vain.

2. It is vain that you rise up early,
sit up late,
and eat the bread of sorrow;
for to him who enjoys his favor,
he gives while he sleeps.

3. Lo, children are a heritage from the Lord,
the fruit of the womb is a reward.

4. Like arrows in the hand of a warrior,
so are the children of youth.

5. Happy is the man who has
his quiver full of them;
They shall not be put to shame
when they speak with their enemies in the gate.

First we must understand that "building the house" does not refer simply to the construction of walls and roof, rooms and chambers, out of wood and stone. It refers rather to everything that goes on inside the house, which in German we call "managing the household" [*haushallten*]; just as Aristotle writes, "*Oeconomia,*" that, is pertaining to the household economy which comprises wife and child, servant and maid, livestock and fodder. The same term is used by Moses in Exodus 1[:20–21], where he writes that God dealt well with the two midwives and "built them houses" because they feared him and did not strangle the children of the Israelites; that is, he helped them to obtain husbands, sons and daughters, and enough of whatever goes along with keeping a family. Solomon's purpose is to describe a Christian marriage; he is instructing everyone how to conduct himself as a Christian husband and head of a household.

Reason and the world think that married life and the making of a home ought to proceed as they intend; they try to determine things by their own decisions and actions, as if their work could take care of everything. To this Solomon says No! He points us instead to God, and teaches us with a firm faith to seek and expect all such things from God. We see this in experience too. Frequently two people will marry who have hardly a shirt to their name, and yet they support themselves so quietly and well that it is a pleasure to behold. On the other hand, some bring great wealth into their marriage; yet it slips out of their hands till they can barely get along.

Again, two people marry out of passionate love; their choice and desire are realized, yet their days together are not happy. Some are very eager and anxious to have children, but they do not conceive, while others who have given the matter little thought get a house full of children. Again, some try to run the house and its servants smoothly, and it turns out that they have nothing but misfortune. And so it goes in this world; the strangest things happen.

Who is it that so disrupts marriage and household management, and turns them so strangely topsy-turvy? It is he of whom Solomon says: Unless the Lord keeps the house, household management there is a lost cause. He wishes to buttress this passage (Ps 127:1a) and confirm its truth. This is why he permits such situations to arise in this world, as an assault on unbelief, to bring to shame the arrogance of reason with all works and cleverness, and to constrain them to believe.

This passage alone should be enough to attract people to marriage, comfort all who are now married, and sap the strength of covetousness. Young people are scared away from marriage when they see how strangely it turns out. They say, "It takes a lot to make a home"; or, "You learn a lot living with a woman." This is because they fail to see who does this, and why He does it; and since human ingenuity and strength know no recourse and can provide no help, they hesitate to marry. As a result they fall into unchastity if they do not marry, and into covetousness and worry if they do. But here is the needed consolation: Let the Lord build the house and keep it, and do not encroach upon his work; the concern for these matters is his, not yours. For whoever is the head of the house and maintains it should be allowed to bear the burden of care. Does it take a lot to make a house? So what! God is greater than any house. He who fills heaven and earth will surely also be able to supply a house, especially since he takes the responsibility upon himself and causes it to be sung to his praise.

Why should we think it strange that it takes so much to make a home where God is not the head of the house? Because you do not see Him who is supposed to fill the house, naturally every corner must seem empty. But if you look upon Him, you will never notice whether a corner is bare; everything will appear to you to be full, and will indeed be full. And if it is not full, it is your vision which is at fault; just as it is the blind man's fault if he fails to see the sun. For him who sees rightly, God turns the saying around and says not, "It takes a lot to make a home," but, "How much a home contributes!" So we see that the managing of a household should and must be done in faith—then there will be enough—so that men come to acknowledge that everything depends not on our doing, but on God's blessing and support.

We are not to understand from this that God forbids us to work. Man must and ought to work, ascribing his sustenance and the fullness of his house, however, not to his own labor but solely to the goodness and blessing of God. For where men ascribe these things to their own labor, there covetousness and anxiety quickly arise, and they hope by much labor to acquire much. But then there is this contradiction, namely, that some people labor prodigiously, yet scarcely have enough to eat, while others are slower and more relaxed in their work, and wealth pours in on them. All this is because God wants the glory, as the one who alone gives the growth (1 Cor 8:6–7). For if you should till the soil faithfully for a hundred years and do all the work in the world, you couldn't bring forth from the earth even a single stalk; but God without any of your labor, while you sleep, produces from that tiny kernel a stalk with as many kernels on it as he wills.

Solomon here wishes to sanction work, but to reject worry and covetousness. He does not say, "The Lord builds the house, so no one need labor at it." He does say,

"Unless the Lord builds the house, those who build it labor in vain" (Ps 127:1a). This is as if he were to say: Man must work, but that work is in vain if it stands alone and thinks it can sustain itself. Work cannot do this; God must do it. Therefore work in such manner that your labor is not in vain. Your labor is in vain when you worry, and rely on your own efforts to sustain yourself. It [is fitting for you] to labor, but your sustenance and the maintenance of your household belong to God alone. Therefore, you must keep these two things far apart: "to labor," and "to maintain a household" or "to sustain"; keep them as far apart from one another as heaven and earth, or God and man.

In the Proverbs of Solomon we often read how the lazy are punished because they will not work. Solomon says, "A slack hand causes poverty, but industrious hands bring riches" (Prov 10:4). This and similar sayings sound as if our sustenance depended on our labor; though he says in the same passage (Prov 10:22), as also in this psalm (127:1), that it depends on God's blessing; or, as we say in German, "God bestows, God provides." Thus, the meaning is this: God commanded Adam to eat his bread in the sweat of his face (Gen 8:19). God wills that man should work, and without work He will give him nothing. Conversely, God will not give him anything because of his labor, but solely out of His own goodness and blessing. Man's labor is to be his discipline in this life, by which he may keep his flesh in subjection. To him who is obedient in this matter, God will give plenty, and sustain him well.

"Unless the Lord builds the house,
those who build it labor in vain."

God sustains man in the same way he sustains all other living creatures. As the psalm (147:9) says, "He gives to all flesh their food, and to the young ravens which cry unto him." Again, in Psalm 104, "The eyes of all look to you, O Lord, and you give them their food in due season. You open your hand, and fill every living creature with blessings," that is, with fullness and sufficiency. Now no animal works for its living, but each has its own task to perform, after which it seeks and finds its food. The little birds fly about and warble, make nests, and hatch their young. That is their task. But they do not gain their living from it. Oxen plow, horses carry their riders and have a share in battle; sheep furnish wool, milk, cheese, etc. That is their task. But they do not gain their living from it. It is the earth which produces grass and nourishes them through God's blessing. Christ himself, in Matthew 6[:26], bids us look at the birds: how they neither sow, nor reap, nor gather into barns; yet they are fed by God.

That is, they perform their tasks all right, but they do no work from which they gain sustenance.

Similarly, man must necessarily work and busy himself at something. At the same time, however, he must know that it is something other than his labor which furnishes him sustenance; it is the divine blessing. Because God gives him nothing unless he works, it may seem as if it is his labor which sustains him; just as the little birds neither sow nor reap, but they would certainly die of hunger if they did not fly about to seek their food. The fact that they find food, however, is not due to their own labor, but to God's goodness. For who placed their food there where they can find it? Beyond all doubt it is God alone, as he says in Genesis 1[:29–30], "Behold, I have given to you and to all creatures every growing plant for food." In short, even if Scripture did not teach this directly, experience would prove it to be so. For where God has not laid up a supply no one will find anything, even though they all work themselves to death searching. We can see this with our eyes, and grasp it with our hands; yet we will not believe. Again, where God does not uphold and preserve, nothing can last, even though a hundred thousand fortresses were thrown up to defend it; it will be shattered and ground to dust till no one knows what has become of it.

Tell me: who puts silver and gold in the mountains so that man might find them there? Who puts into the field that great wealth which issues in grain, wine, and all kinds of produce, from which all creatures live? Does the labor of man do this? To be sure, labor no doubt finds it, but God has first to bestow it and put it there if labor is to find it.

Who puts into the flesh the power to bring forth young and fill the earth with birds, beasts, fish, etc.? Is this accomplished by our labor and care? By no means. God is there first, secretly laying his blessing therein; then all things are brought forth in abundance. And so we find that all our labor is nothing more than the finding and collecting of God's gifts; it is quite unable to create or preserve anything.

Here then we see how Solomon, in this one little verse (Ps 127:1), has solved in short order the greatest of all problems among the children of men, about which so many books have been written, so many proverbs and approaches devised, namely, how to feed our poor stomachs. Solomon rejects them all in a body, wraps the whole matter up in faith, and says: You labor in vain when you labor for the purpose of sustaining yourself and building your own house. Indeed, you make for yourself a lot of worry, and trouble. At the same time by such arrogance and wicked unbelief you kindle God's wrath, so that you only become all the poorer and are mined completely because you undertook to do what is his alone to do. And if with such unbelief you should succeed anyway in attaining wealth in all things, it would only bring greater ruin to your soul eternally when God lets you go blindly on in your unbelief.

If you want to earn your livelihood honorably, quietly, and well, and rightly maintain your household, give heed: Take up some occupation that will keep you busy in order that you can eat your bread in the sweat of your face (Gen 3:19). Then do not worry about how you will be sustained and how such labor will build and maintain your house. Place everything in God's keeping; let him do the worrying and the building. Entrust these things to him; he will lay before you richly and well the things which your labor is to find and bring to you. If he does not put them there, you will labor in vain and find nothing.

Thus, this wholly evangelical [gospel] verse in masterful fashion sets forth faith, as against that accursed covetousness and concern for the belly which today, alas! everywhere hinders the fruit of the gospel.

When this verse is fully understood, the rest of the psalm is easy. We will now briefly run through the other verses.

> Unless the Lord keeps the city,
> the watchman guards in vain.

In the first verse he rebuked covetousness, worry, and unbelief in every household in particular. In this verse he does the same thing for a whole community. For a whole community is nothing other than many households combined. By this term we comprehend all manner of principalities, dominions, and kingdoms, or any other grouping of people.

Now the blind world, because it does not know God and his work, concludes that it is owing to its own cleverness, reason, and strength that a community or dominion endures and thrives. Accordingly, they gather together great treasures, stuff their coffers, construct mighty towers and walls, provide suits of armor and vast supplies of provisions, enact wise laws, and conduct their affairs with courage and prudence. They just go ahead in their arrogance without even consulting God about any of it, like those who built the Tower of Babel (Gen 11:1–9).

Meanwhile, God sits above and watches how cleverly and boldly the children of men proceed, and he causes the psalmist to sing in his praise, "God brings the counsel of the nations to naught" (Ps 33:10). Again, "God knows the thoughts of man, that they are vain" (Ps 94:11). And yet again, "He takes away the spirit of princes, and deals strongly with the kings of the earth" (Ps 76:12). He allows such cities and dominions to arise and to gain the ascendancy, for a little while. But before they can look around he strikes them down; and in general the greater the kingdom, the sooner. Even though they flourish for a short time, that is in the sight of God little more than a beginning. Never does one of them arrive at the point it strives to reach.

If you will look at the history of the kingdoms of Assyria, Babylon, Persia, Greece, Rome, and all the rest, you will find there exactly what this verse says. All their splendor is nothing more than God's little puppet show. He has allowed them to rise for a time, but he has invariably overthrown them, one after the other. As they gained a brief ascendancy, through human wit and arrogance, so much the more quickly did they fall again; not because they lacked manpower, money, goods, and all manner of resources, but because the true watchman had ceased to uphold them, and caused them to see what human wit and power could accomplish without his watchful care and protection. So it turned out that their cause was nothing but vain counsel and a futile undertaking which they could neither uphold nor carry out.

. . . One of two things must necessarily follow when we rely on our own watchfulness: either arrogance or worry. If all goes well and is secure, we pride ourselves on our watchfulness; if things go wrong and are about to fail, we worry, lose heart, and become doubtful. Now God will tolerate neither of these, neither arrogance nor worry. We should neither worry when we are insecure, nor be proud when we are secure, but in free and true faith do our watching and perform the duties of our calling. We should no more be anxious when things go wrong than be proud when things go well . . .

Why, then, does he urge us to labor and watch, and want us to have walls, armor, and all manner of supplies, just as he commanded the children of Israel to put on their armor and fight against the Canaanites? Are we to provide no supplies, leave our gates and windows open, make no effort to defend ourselves but allow ourselves to be pierced through and become lifeless corpses as they did in the book of Maccabees? (1 Macc[2] 2:34–38). By no means. You have just heard that those in authority should be watchful and diligent, and perform all the duties of their office: bar the gates, defend the towers and walls, put on armor, and procure supplies. In general, they should proceed as if there were no God and they had to rescue themselves and manage their own affairs; just as the head of a household is supposed to work as if he were trying to sustain himself by his own labors.

But he must watch out that his heart does not come to rely on these deeds of his, and get arrogant when things go well or worried when things go wrong. He should

---

2   1 and 2 Maccabees – two books of the Apocrypha, a collection of books included in the Roman Catholic Bible

regard all such preparation and equipment as being the work of our Lord God under a mask, as it were, beneath which he himself alone effects and accomplishes what we desire . . . Indeed, one could very well say that the course of the world, and especially the doing of his saints, are God's mask, under which he conceals himself and so marvelously exercises dominion and introduces disorder in the world.

> It is vain that you rise up early
> and go to bed late,
> and eat the bread of sorrow;
> for so he gives to his beloved in sleep.

This whole verse (Ps 127:2) is directed against arrogance and anxiety, as if he were to say: It is futile for you to rise up early and go to bed late, and think that the more you labor the more you will have. For that is something that the blessing of God has to accomplish. And even if you do succeed in acquiring more than others who are not so concerned about getting things and keeping them, still your earnings will not go as far as those of the carefree, but will slip through your fingers and disappear, as Psalm 37[:16] says, "It is better for the righteous to have a little than to have the great riches of the wicked." And Solomon says in the Proverbs, "Better is a dinner of herbs where love is, than a fatted ox and hatred with it" (Prov 15:17).

That this is his meaning, and that it is not his intent to prohibit labor or diligence, is clear from his phrase, "and eat the bread of sorrow." This says in effect: You are making your bread and sustenance harsh and bitter; and this is not the fault of your labor, but of your anxious and unbelieving heart. It refuses to believe that God will nourish you; instead, it is importunate and demanding, wanting to fill coffers, purses, cellars, and storehouses, and refusing to rest until it is assured of having more supplies on hand than it could consume in many years. He who has faith in God, however, is not anxious about tomorrow but is content with today. He does his work with joy and with a quiet heart, and lives in accord with Christ's injunction in the gospel, "Do not be anxious about tomorrow, for tomorrow will have its own troubles. It is enough that each day has its own evil." Lo, the livelihood of such believers will not be harsh and bitter; for although they too eat their bread in the sweat of their faces outwardly (Gen 3:19), they do it with faith and a joyful conscience inwardly.

Thereupon, he concludes by showing how God gives all such things, saying: All such things (both the building of the house and the keeping of the city) he gives to his beloved as in their sleep (Ps 127:2). That is, he lets them work hard and be diligent, in such a way, however, that they are neither anxious nor arrogant, but go happily along, assuming no burden of care, and committing everything to Him. They live a calm and untroubled life with tranquil hearts, as one who sleeps sweetly and securely, letting nothing trouble him, and yet continues to live and be well cared for. They have enough; indeed, they must be well supplied and protected because they have committed all to God in accordance with Psalm 55[:22], "Cast your burden on the Lord, and he will sustain you"; and I Peter 5[:7], "Cast all your anxieties on him, and know that he cares for you." At issue is not the matter of work, but only the matter of pernicious worry, covetousness, and unbelief.

> Lo, children are a heritage from the Lord,
> the fruit of the womb a reward.

All of this is spoken in typical Hebrew fashion. "Heritage from the Lord" and "reward" are one and the same thing, just as "children" and "fruit of the womb" are one and the same thing. Thus it means to say: What good does it do you to be so deeply concerned and anxious about how to procure and protect your possessions? Why even children, and whatever is born of woman, are not within your power; although they are a part of household and city alike, for if there were no children and "fruit of the womb" neither household nor city would endure. So the very reward and "heritage from the Lord," about which you are so terribly anxious, are actually the gift and boon of God. (Even if all the whole world were to combine forces, they could not bring about the conception of a single child in any woman's womb nor cause it to be born; that is wholly the work of God alone.) Why, then, are you concerned and anxious about acquiring and securing goods, when you do not even possess that for which you seek them? A lord, then, and the head of a household ought rightfully to say to himself: I will labor and perform my allotted tasks; but He who creates children in the home and inhabitants in the city (all of whom are "fruit of the womb") will also sustain and preserve them. Lo, this one's labor and that one's watching would then not be bitter to him, but would proceed aright in faith.

Christ touched upon this (to which virtually the whole psalm is devoted) when he said in Matthew 8[:25],

"Is not the body more than clothing, and the soul more than food.?" It is as if he were to say: Since children and "the fruit of the womb" are not for you to worry about, why then do you worry about the matter of securing and keeping possessions? For who can ever explain how it is that all the children of men are brought forth out of the flesh of women? Who has hidden such a multitude of men in that poor flesh, and who brings them forth in such marvelous fashion? None other than He alone, who gives children as a heritage and the fruit of the womb as a reward to his beloved (Ps 127:3) as in sleep (Ps 127:2). God bestows his gifts overnight, they say; and that is literally true.

> Like arrows in the hand of a warrior,
> so are the children of one's youth.

Here he compares children and people with the arrows in the hand of a mighty hero, who shoots his arrows whenever and withersoever he wills. Thus, we also see how God deals with us. Just look at how amazingly he matches husband and wife, in a way no one would expect; and how they attain to extraordinary stations in life for which they have not striven, so that men marvel at it. Generally, things turn out quite differently from what father, and mother, and even the person himself, had envisioned. It is as if God would confess this verse (Ps 127:4) in deeds and say: I will bring to naught all the counsels of men and deal with the children of men according to my own will, that they may be in my hand as the arrows of a powerful giant. Of what use is a lot of worrying and planning for our future when that future will be nothing other than

what he wills? The best thing to do then is to work and
let him worry about the future . . .

> Happy is the man who has
> his quiver full of them;
> They shall not be put to shame
> when they speak with their enemies in the gate.

. . . Such a great blessing however, will not be without
persecution, for where things go according to God's will
there must also be onslaughts of the devil. The unbelief
and covetousness of this world cannot tolerate godly life
and teaching; therefore, such householders and cities
will not be without enemies to revile and abuse them. But
over against such attacks there stands this comfort, that
they will ultimately emerge with honor and put their
enemies to shame in the gate (that is, publicly) (Ps 127:5).
He mentions no armor or weapons but only the word,
saying that "they will speak with their enemies in the gate,"
as if to say: By their teaching they will stand, because it
is true, no matter how sharply their opponents attack it.

I wanted to write this to you, my dear friends in Christ,
for your encouragement, that your hearts and ours
may be yet more diligent, in order that the gospel may
become rich and fruitful among us all in all manner
of understanding and of good works, against which
covetousness, the fruit of pernicious unbelief, fights
so vigorously. Our dear Lord Jesus Christ strengthen
and help us. For if we are still so weak that we cannot
leave off worrying about the needs of our bellies, how
shall we be able to bear the world's fury, death,
[criticism] and all other misfortune? Yes, how shall
we stand firm when the false spirits come upon us,

who just now are beginning to rise? May God, the Father of all mercy, who has introduced his word and begun his work among you, preserve your minds and hearts in the simple and pure knowledge of Jesus Christ our Savior, to whom be praise and thanks in all eternity. Amen.

Discussion Questions

 Luther talks about something called the *oeconomia*: the household economy. How does this differ from the way you understand households today? How does it differ from the way you think about the economy?

 How does Luther expand his reflections on the family to include society and government? How does he think about each of these systems as a "house"? How does this connect to Psalm 127?

 Luther says that covetousness, arrogance, and worry come from humans relying on their own watchfulness. How does he connect these different postures? In what ways are you experiencing greed, pride, or anxiety?

 Why does Luther say we should work? What role does your work play in relation to God's creation and provision?

 Luther says some have a lot and some have a little. Why does he think this is the case? What practices can you be cultivating in regard to your own household finances? Giving? Work? Investments?

Chapter 7

Abolition and Liberation

But he who with a view to self-exaltation causes some with their domestic animals to labor immoderately, and with the moneys arising to him therefrom employs others in the luxuries of life, acts contrary to the gracious design of him who is the true owner of the earth.

~ John Woolman

I can count on the fingers of one hand the number of times that I have heard a sermon on the meaning of religion, of Christianity, to the man who stands with his back against the wall. It is urgent that my meaning be crystal clear. The masses of men live with their backs constantly against the wall. They are the poor, the disinherited, the dispossessed. What does our religion say to them?

~ Howard Thurman

JOHN WOOLMAN (1720–1772)

Background

John Woolman was a Quaker minister who argued against the slave trade and injustices related to the seizure of Native American lands. He lived simply and worked with his hands, refusing to wear clothing connected with forced human labor and advocating for reparations for African American freed people. As a Quaker, he practiced and preached nonviolence. Because of the work of Woolman and Benjamin Lay, among others, the Quakers adopted and maintained an abolitionist stance, often participating in the Underground Railroad.

In *A Plea for the Poor*, Woolman points to the systemic nature of injustice and pleads with Christians to consider how their own economic practices contribute to or detract from the poverty of others. Like Aquinas and Luther, he argues from the good of creation to the necessity of sharing goods with all. Like Basil and Chrysostom, he sees accumulation of wealth as theft from the poor. Like Clare and Catherine, he extols the virtues of living simply. Woolman's work is an important contribution to the tradition of thinking about Christian mission and poverty. Unlike many contemporary Christians, Woolman refuses to think about poverty in purely individualistic or purely systemic terms. He calls for a commitment to both Jesus and justice in a way that we would do well to learn from today.

Text

A Plea for the Poor, or a Word of Remembrance and Caution to the Rich

1. Section One

Wealth desired for its own sake obstructs the increase of virtue, and large possessions in the hands of selfish men have a bad tendency, for by their means too small a number of people are employed in things useful; and therefore they, or some of them, are necessitated to labor too hard, while others would want business to earn their bread were not employments invented which, having no real use, serve only to please the vain mind. Rents set on lands are often so high that persons who have but small substance are straitened in hiring a plantation; and while tenants are healthy and prosperous in business, they often find occasion to labor harder than was intended by our gracious Creator. Oxen and horses are often seen at work when, through heat and too much labor, their eyes and the emotion of their bodies manifest that they are oppressed. Their loads in wagons are frequently so heavy that when weary with hauling it far, their drivers find occasion in going up hills or through mire to raise their spirits by whipping to get forward.

Many poor people are so thronged in their business that it is difficult for them to provide shelter suitable for their animals in great storms. These things are common when in health, but through sickness and inability to labor, through loss of creatures and miscarriage in business, many are straitened; and so much of their increase goes annually to pay rent or interest that they have not wherewith to hire so much as their case requires. Hence one poor woman, in attending on her children, providing for her family, and helping the sick, does as much business as would for the time be suitable employment for two or three; and honest persons are often straitened to give their children suitable learning. The money which the wealthy receive from the poor, who do more than a proper share of business in raising it, is frequently paid to other poor people for doing business which is foreign to the true use of things.

Men who have large possessions and live in the spirit of charity, who carefully inspect the circumstance of those who occupy their estates, and regardless of the customs of the times regulate their demands agreeable to universal love, these, by being righteous on a principle, do good to the poor without placing it as an act of bounty. Their example in avoiding superfluities tends to incite others to moderation. Their goodness in not exacting what the laws or customs would support them in tends to open the channel to moderate labor in useful affairs and to discourage those branches of business which have not their foundation in true wisdom. To be busied in that which is but vanity and serves only to please the unstable mind tends to an alliance with them who promote that vanity, and is a snare in which many poor tradesmen are entangled. To be employed in things connected with virtue is most agreeable to the character and inclination of an honest man. While industrious, frugal people are borne down with poverty and oppressed with too much labor in useful things, the way to apply money without promoting pride and vanity remains open to such who truly sympathize with them in their various difficulties.

2. Section Two

The Creator of the earth is the owner of it. He gave us being thereon, and our nature requires nourishment which is the produce of it. As he is kind and merciful, we as his creatures, while we live answerable to the design of our creation, we are so far entitled to a convenient subsistence that no man may justly deprive us of it. By the agreements and contracts of our fathers and predecessors, and by doings and proceedings of our own, some claim a much greater share of this world than others; and while those possessions are faithfully improved to the good of the whole, it consists with equity. But he who with a view to self-exaltation causes some with their domestic animals to labor immoderately, and with the moneys arising to him therefrom employs others in the luxuries of life, acts contrary to the gracious design of him who is the true owner of the earth; nor can any possessions, either acquired or derived from ancestors, justify such conduct.

Goodness remains to be goodness, and the direction of pure wisdom is obligatory on all reasonable creatures— that laws and customs are no further a standard for our proceedings than as their foundation is on universal righteousness. Though the poor occupy our estates by a bargain to which they in their poor circumstance agreed, and we ask even less than a punctual fulfilling of their agreement, yet if our views are to lay up riches or to live in conformity to customs which have not their foundation in the Truth, and our demands are such as requires greater toil or application to business in them than is consistent with pure love, we invade their rights as inhabitants of that world of which a good and gracious God is proprietor, under whom we are tenants. Were all

superfluities and the desire of outward greatness laid aside and the right use of things universally attended to, such a number of people might be employed in things useful that moderate labor with the blessing of heaven would answer all good purposes relating to people and their animals, and a sufficient number have leisure to attend on proper affairs of civil society.

3. Section Three

While our strength and spirits are lively, we go cheerfully through business. Either too much or too little action is tiresome, but a right portion is healthful to our bodies and agreeable to an honest mind. Where men have great estates they stand in a place of trust. To have it in their power without difficulty to live in that fashion which occasions much labor, and at the same time confine themselves to that use of things prescribed by our Redeemer, and confirmed by his example and the example of many who lived in the early ages of the Christian church, that they may more extensively relieve objects of charity—for men possessed of great estates to live thus requires close attention to divine love. Our gracious Creator cares and provides for all his creatures. His tender mercies are over all his works; and so far as his love influences our minds, so far we become interested in his workmanship and feel a desire to take hold of every opportunity to lessen the distresses of the afflicted and increase the happiness of the creation. Here we have a prospect of one common interest from which our own is inseparable—that to turn all the treasures we possess into the channel of universal love becomes the business of our lives . . .

Poor men eased of their burdens and released from too
close an application to business are at liberty to hire others
to their assistance, to provide well for their animals, and
find time to perform those visits amongst their acquaintance
which belongs to a well-guided social life. When these
reflect on the opportunity those had to oppress them, and
consider the goodness of their conduct, they behold it
lovely and consistent with brotherhood; and as the man
whose mind is conformed to universal love has his trust
settled in God and finds a firm foundation to stand on in
any changes or revolutions that happen amongst men,
so also the goodness of his conduct tends to spread a kind,
benevolent disposition in the world.

4. Section Four

Our blessed Redeemer, in directing us how to conduct one
towards another, appeals to our own feeling: "Whatever
you would that other men should do to you, do you even
so to them" (Matt 7:12). Now where such live in fullness
on the labor of others, who have never had experience of
hard labor themselves, there is often a danger of their
not having a right feeling of the laborer's condition, and
therefore of being disqualified to judge candidly in their
case, not knowing what they themselves would desire were
they to labor hard from one year to another to raise the
necessaries of life and to pay large rents beside—that it's
good for those who live in fullness to labor for tenderness
of heart, to improve every opportunity of being acquainted
with the hardships and fatigues of those who labor for
their living, and [to] think seriously with themselves: Am
I influenced with true charity in fixing all my demands?
Have I no desire to support myself in expensive customs
because my acquaintance live in those customs, Were

I to labor as they do toward supporting them and their children in a station like mine, in such sort as they and their children labor for us, could I not on such a change, before I entered into agreements of rents or interest, name some costly articles now used by me or in my family which have no real use in them, the expense whereof might be lessened? And should I not in such case strongly desire the disuse of those needless expenses, that less answering their way of life the terms might be the easier to me?

If a wealthy man, on serious reflection, finds a witness in his own conscience that there are some expenses which he indulges himself in that are in conformity to custom, which might be omitted consistent with the true design of living, and which was he to change places with those who occupy his estate he would desire to be discontinued by them—whoever are thus awakened to their feeling will necessarily find the injunction binding on them: "Do you even so to them." Divine love imposes no rigorous or unreasonable commands, but graciously points out the spirit of brotherhood and way to happiness, in the attaining to which it is necessary that we go forth out of all that is selfish.

5. Section Five

To pass through a series of hardships and to languish under oppression brings people to a certain knowledge of these things. To enforce the duty of tenderness to the poor, the inspired Lawgiver referred the children of Israel to their own past experience: "Ye know the heart of a stranger, seeing ye were strangers in the land of Egypt" (Exod 23:9). He who has been a stranger amongst unkind people or under their government who were hard-hearted, knows how it feels; but a person who has never felt the weight of misapplied power comes not to this knowledge but by an inward tenderness, in which the heart is prepared to sympathize with others. We may reflect on the condition of a poor, innocent man, who by his labor contributes toward supporting one of his own species more wealthy than himself, on whom the rich man from a desire after wealth and luxuries lays heavy burdens.

When this laborer looks over the means of his heavy load, and considers that this great toil and fatigue is laid on him to support that which has no foundation in pure wisdom, we may well suppose that there arises an uneasiness in his mind toward those who might without any inconvenience deal more favorably with him. When he considers that by his industry his fellow creature is benefited, and sees that this man who has much wealth is not satisfied with being supported in a plain way—but to gratify a wrong desire and conform to wrong customs, increases to an extreme the labors of those who occupy his estate—we may reasonably judge that he will think himself unkindly used. When he considers that the proceedings of the wealthy are agreeable to the customs of the times, and sees no means of redress in this world, how would the inward sighing of an innocent person ascend to the throne of that great, good Being, who created us all and has a constant care over his creatures.

By candidly considering these things, we may have some sense of the condition of innocent people overloaded by the wealthy. But he who toils one year after another to furnish others with wealth and superfluities, who labors and thinks, and thinks and labors, till by overmuch labor he is wearied and oppressed, such an one understands

the meaning of that language: "You know the heart of
a stranger, seeing you were strangers in the land of Egypt."
As many at this day who know not the heart of a stranger
indulge themselves in ways of life which occasions more
labor in the world than Infinite Goodness intends for
man, and yet are compassionate toward such in distress
who comes directly under their observation, were these
to change circumstances a while with some who labor for
them, were they to pass regularly through the means
of knowing the heart of a stranger and come to a feeling
knowledge of the straits and hardships which many
poor, innocent people pass through in a hidden obscure
life, were these who now fare sumptuously every day to
act the other part of the scene till seven times had passed
over them, and return again to their former estate, I believe
many of them would embrace a way of life less expensive
and lighten the heavy burdens of some who now labor
out of their sight to support them and pass through straits
with which they are but little acquainted.

To see our fellow creatures under difficulties to which
we are in no degree accessory tends to awaken tenderness
in the minds of all reasonable people, but if we consider
the condition of such who are depressed in answering our
demands, who labor out of our sight and are often toiling
for us while we pass our time in fullness, if we consider
that much less than we demand would supply us with all
things really needful, what heart will not relent, or what
reasonable man can refrain from mitigating that grief which
he himself is the cause of, when he may do it without
inconvenience? I shall conclude with the words of Ezekiel
the prophet (Chap. 34, verse 18), "Seems it a small [thing

unto you to have eaten up the poor pasture, but ye must tread down with your feet the residue of your pastures?]"

6. Section Six

People much spent with labor often take strong drink to revive them. Were there more men usefully employed and fewer who eat bread as a reward for doing that which is not useful, then food or raiment would, on a reasonable estimate, be more in proportion to labor than it is at present. In proceeding agreeable to sound wisdom, a small portion of daily labor might suffice to keep a proper stream gently circulating through all the channels of society; and this portion of labor might be so divided and taken in the most advantageous parts of the day that people would not have that plea for the use of strong liquors which they have at present . . .

When people are spent with action and take these liquors not only as a refreshment from past labors but to support them to go on without nature having sufficient time to recruit by resting, it gradually turns them from that calmness of thought which attends those who steadily apply their hearts to true wisdom. The spirits scattered by too much bodily motion in the heat and again revived by strong drink—that this makes a person unfit for serious thinking and divine meditation I expect will not be denied; and as multitudes of people are in this practice who do not take so much as to hinder them from managing their outward affairs, this custom requires our serious thoughts . . .

By too much labor the spirits are exhausted and people crave help from strong drink; and the frequent use of strong drink works in opposition to the Holy Spirit on the mind. This is plain when men take so much as to suspend the use of their reason, and though there are degrees of this opposition, and a man quite drunk may be furthest removed from that frame of mind in which God is acceptably worshiped, yet a person being often near spent with too much action and revived by spirituous liquors without being quite drunk inures himself to that which is a less degree of the same thing, and which by long continuance does necessarily hurt both mind and body . . .

As many who manifest some regard to piety do yet in some degree conform to those ways of living and of collecting wealth which increases labor beyond the bounds fixed by divine wisdom, my desire is that they may so consider the connection of things as to take heed, lest by exacting of poor men more than is consistent with universal righteousness they promote that by their conduct which in words they speak against. To treasure up wealth for another generation by means of the immoderate labor of such who in some measure depend upon us is doing evil at present, without knowing but that our wealth, thus gathered, may be applied to evil purposes when we are gone . . . Lay aside the profession of a pious life and people expect little or no instruction from the example. But while we profess in all cases to live in constant opposition to that which is contrary to universal righteousness, what expressions are equal to the subject, or what language is sufficient to set forth the strength of those obligations we are under to beware lest by our example we lead others wrong.

7. Section Seven

"This kind goes not out but by prayer" (Matt 11:21). In our care for our children, should we give way to partiality in things relating to what may be when we are gone, yet after death we cannot look at partiality with pleasure. If by our wealth we make them great without a full persuasion that we could not bestow it better, and thus give them power to deal hardly with others more virtuous than they, it can, after death, give us no more satisfaction than if by this treasure we had raised these others above our own and given them power to oppress ours. Did a man possess as much good land as would well suffice twenty industrious, frugal people, and expect that he was lawful heir to it and intend to give this great estate to his children, but found on a research into the title that one-half this estate was the undoubted property of a number of poor orphans who, as to virtue and understanding, to him appeared as hopeful as his own children—this discovery would give him an opportunity to consider whether he was attached to any interest distinct from the interest of those children.

Some of us have estates sufficient for our children and for as many more to live upon did they all employ their time in useful business and live in that plainness consistent with the character of true disciples of Christ, and have no reason to believe that our children after us will apply them to benevolent purposes more than some poor children who we are acquainted with would, if they had them; and yet, did we believe that after our decease these estates would go equally between our children and an equal number of these poor children, it would be likely to give us uneasiness. This may show to a thoughtful person that to be redeemed from all the remains of selfishness, to have a universal regard to our fellow creatures, and love them as our Heavenly Father loves them, we must constantly attend to the influence of his Spirit . . .

As that natural desire of superiority in us, being given way to, extends to such our favorites whom we expect will succeed us, and as the grasping after wealth and power for them adds greatly to the burdens of the poor and increases the evil of covetousness in this age, I have often desired in secret that in looking toward posterity we may remember the purity of that rest which is prepared for the Lord's people, the impossibility of our taking pleasure in anything distinguishable from universal righteousness, and how vain and weak a thing it is to give wealth and power to such who appear unlikely to apply it to a general good when we are gone.

As Christians, all we possess are the gifts of God. Now in distributing it to others we act as his steward, and it becomes our station to act agreeable to that divine wisdom which he graciously gives to his servants . . . For if we, after such settlement and when too late for an alteration, attain to that purified state which our Redeemer prayed his Father that his people might attain to—of being united to the Father and the Son—a sincere repentance for all things done in a will separate from universal love must precede this inward sanctification; and though in such depth of repentance and reconciliation all sins are forgiven and sorrows removed, that our misdeeds heretofore done could no longer afflict us, yet our partial determinations in favor of such whom we loved in a selfish love could not afford us any pleasure. And if after such selfish settlement our wills continue to stand in opposition to the fountain of universal light and love, there will be an impassable gulf between the soul and true felicity, nor can anything heretofore done in this separate will afford us pleasure.

8. Section Eight

To labor for an establishment in divine love where the mind is disentangled from the power of darkness is the great business of man's life. Collecting of riches, covering the body with fine-wrought, costly apparel, and having magnificent furniture operates against universal love and tends to feed self, that to desire these things belongs not to the children of the Light. He who sent ravens to feed Elijah in the wilderness, and increased the poor widow's small remains of meal and oil, is now as attentive to the necessities of his people as ever, that when he numbers us with his people and says, "You are my sons and daughters" (2 Cor 6:18)—no greater happiness can be desired by them who know how gracious a Father he is . . .

Our hearts being thus opened and enlarged, we feel content in a use of things as foreign to luxury and grandeur as that which our Redeemer laid down as a pattern . . . "It is easier," says our Savior, "for a camel to go through a needle's eye than for a rich man to enter the kingdom of God" (Mark 10:25). Here our Lord uses an instructing similitude, for as a camel considered under that character cannot pass through a needle's eye, so a man who trusts in riches and holds them for the sake of the power and distinction attending them cannot in that spirit enter the kingdom.

Now every part of a camel may be so reduced as to pass through a hole as small as a needle's eye, yet such is the bulk of the creature, and the hardness of its bones and teeth, that it could not be completed without much labor. So man must cease from that spirit which craves riches, and be reduced into another disposition, before he inherits the kingdom, as effectually as a camel must cease from the form of a camel in passing through the eye of a needle. When our Savior said to the rich youth, "Go sell that you hast and give to the poor" (Mark 10:21), though undoubtedly it was his duty to have done so, yet to confine this of selling all as a duty on every true Christian would be to limit the Holy One. Obedient children who are entrusted with much outward substance wait for wisdom to dispose of it agreeable to his will, in whom "the fatherless finds mercy" (Hos 14:3).

It may not be the duty of everyone to commit at once their substance to other hands, but rather from time to time to look round amongst the numerous branches of the great family, as his stewards who said, "Leave your fatherless children; I will preserve them alive; and let your widows trust in me" (Jer 49:11). But as disciples of Christ, however entrusted with much goods, they may not conform to sumptuous or luxurious living. For if possessing great treasures had been a sufficient reason to make a fine show in the world, then Christ our Lord, who had an unfailing storehouse, and in a way surpassing the common operations in nature supplied thousands of people with food, would not have lived in so much plainness. What we equitably possess is a gift from God to us; but by the Son all things were created. Now he who forms things out of nothing—who creates and, having created, does possess—is more truly rich than he who possesses by receiving gifts from another.

If depth of knowledge and a high title had been sufficient reasons to make a splendid show, he would have made it. He told the woman of Samaria sundry things relative to her past life, made mention of the decease of Lazarus, and answered the scribe who accounted him a blasphemer, without information, and having the spirit without measure knew what was in man. The title of Lord he owned, nor was it ever more justly given to any—that in riches and wisdom and greatness there was none on earth equal to him; and as he lived in perfect plainness and simplicity, the greatest in his family cannot by virtue of their station claim a right to live in worldly grandeur without contradicting his doctrine who said: "It is enough for the disciple to be as his master" (Matt 10:25).

9. Section Nine

If we consider the havoc that is made in this age, and how numbers of people are hurried on, striving to collect treasures to please that mind which wanders from perfect resignation, and in that wisdom which is foolishness with God are perverting the true use of things, laboring as in the fire, contending with one another even unto blood, and exerting their power to support ways of living foreign to the life of one wholly crucified to the world; if we consider what great numbers of people are employed in different kingdoms in preparing the materials of war, and the labor and toil of armies set apart for protecting their respective territories from the incursions of others, and the extensive miseries which attend their engagements; while many of those who till the lands and are employed in other useful things—in supporting themselves, supporting those employed in military affairs, and some who own the soil—have great hardships to encounter through too

much labor; while others in several kingdoms are busied
in fetching men to help labor from distant parts of
the world, to spend the remainder of their lives in the
uncomfortable condition of slaves, and that self is at the
bottom of these proceedings—amidst all this confusion,
and these scenes of sorrow and distress, can we remember
the Prince of Peace, remember that we are his disciples,
and remember that example of humility and plainness
which he set for us, without feeling an earnest desire to
be disentangled from everything connected with selfish
customs in food, in raiment, in houses, and all things else;
that being of Christ['s] family and walking as he walked,
we may stand in that uprightness wherein man was first
made, and have no fellowship with those inventions
which men in the fallen wisdom have sought out.

In the selfish spirit stands idolatry. Did our blessed
Redeemer enable his family to endure great reproaches,
and suffer cruel torments even unto death, for their
testimony against the idolatry of those times; and can
we behold the prevalence of idolatry though under
a different appearance, without being jealous over ourselves
lest we unwarily join in it? Those faithful martyrs refused
to cast incense into the fire, though by doing it they might
have escaped a cruel death. Casting sweet-scented matter
into the fire to make a comfortable smell—this considered
separate from all circumstances—would appear to be of
small consequence; but as they would thereby have signified
their approbation of idolatry, it was necessarily refused
by the faithful. Nor can we in any degree depart from pure
universal righteousness and publicly continue in that
which is not agreeable to the Truth, without strengthening
the hands of the unrighteous and doing that which in the
nature of the thing is like offering incense to an idol . . .

10. Section Ten

"Are not two sparrows sold for a farthing, and one of them shall not fall on the ground without your Father" (Matt 10:29). The way of carrying on wars, common in the world, is so far distinguishable from the purity of Christ's religion that many scruple to join in them. Those who are so redeemed from the love of the world as to possess nothing in a selfish spirit, their "life is hid with Christ in God" (Col 3:3), and these he preserves in resignation, even in times of commotion. As they possess nothing but what pertains to his family, anxious thoughts about wealth or dominion has little or nothing in them to work upon, and they learn contentment in being disposed of according to his will who, being omnipotent and always mindful of his children, causes all things to work for their good.

But where that spirit which loves riches works, and in its working gathers wealth and cleaves to customs which have their root in self-pleasing, this spirit, thus separating from universal love, seeks help from that power which stands in the separation; and whatever name it has, it still desires to defend the treasures thus gotten. This is like a chain where the end of one link encloses the end of another. The rising up of a desire to attain wealth is the beginning. This desire being cherished moves to action, and riches thus gotten please self, and while self has a life in them it desires to have them defended.

Wealth is attended with power, by which bargains and proceedings contrary to universal righteousness are supported; and here oppression, carried on with worldly policy and order, clothes itself with the name of justice and becomes like a seed of discord in the soil; and as this spirit which wanders from the pure habitation prevails, so the seed of war swells and sprouts and grows and becomes strong, till much fruits are ripened. Thus comes the harvest spoken of by the prophet, which is "a heap in the day of grief, and of desperate sorrow" (Isa 17:11).

Oh, that we who declare against wars and acknowledge our trust to be in God only, may walk in the Light and therein examine our foundation and motives in holding great estates! May we look upon our treasures and the furniture of our houses and the garments in which we array ourselves and try whether the seeds of war have any nourishment in these our possessions or not. Holding treasures in the self-pleasing spirit is a strong plant, the fruit whereof ripens fast. A day of outward distress is coming and divine love calls to prepare against it! Harken then, Oh you children who have known the Light, and come forth! Leave everything which our Lord Jesus Christ does not own. Think not his pattern too plain or too coarse for you. Think not a small portion in this life too little, but let us live in his spirit and walk as he walked, and he will preserve us in the greatest troubles.

11. Section Eleven

"The heavens, even the heavens, are the Lord's, but the earth has he given to the children of men" (Ps 115:16). As servants of God, what land or estate we hold, we hold under him as his gift; and in applying the profits it is our duty to act consistent with the design of our benefactor. Imperfect men may give on motives of misguided affection, but Perfect Wisdom and Goodness gives agreeable to his own nature. Nor is this gift absolute, but conditional, for us to occupy as dutiful children and not otherwise, for he alone is the proprietor. "The world," says he, "is mine, and the fullness thereof" (Ps 24:1).

The inspired Lawgiver directed that such of the Israelites who sold their inheritance should sell it for a term only, and that they or their children should again enjoy it in the Year of Jubilee, settled on every fiftieth year. "The land shall not be sold forever, for the land is mine," says the Lord, "for you are strangers and sojourners with me" (Lev 25:23), the design of which was to prevent the rich from oppressing the poor by too much engrossing the land. And our blessed Redeemer said: "Till heaven and earth pass, one jot or one tittle shall in no wise pass from the law till all be fulfilled" (Matt 5:18).

Where divine love takes place in the hearts of any people, and they steadily act on a principle of universal righteousness, there the true intent of the Law is fulfilled, though their outward modes of proceeding may be distinguishable from one another. But where men are possessed by that spirit hinted at by the prophet, and looking over their wealth, say in their hearts, "Have we not taken to us horns by our own strength?" (Amos 6:13)—here they deviate from the divine law and do not account their possessions so strictly God's, nor the weak and poor entitled to so much of the increase thereof, but that they may indulge their desires in conforming to worldly pomp. And thus where house is joined to house and field laid to field till there is no place, and the poor are thereby straitened, though this be done by bargain and purchase, yet, so far as it stands distinguished from universal love, so far that woe prefixed by the prophet will accompany their proceedings.

As he who first formed the earth out of nothing was then the true proprietor of it, so he still remains; and though he has given it to the children of men, so that multitudes of people have had sustenance from it while they continued here, yet he has never aliened it; but his right to give is as good as at the first, nor can any apply the increase of their possessions contrary to universal love, nor dispose of lands in a way which they know tends to exalt some by oppressing others, without being justly chargeable with [rebellion] . . .

HOWARD THURMAN (1899–1981)

Background

In many ways, Howard Thurman provided the theological framework for the American civil rights movement. In addition to his role in advising leaders of various social justice organizations, his masterwork *Jesus and the Disinherited* was of such significance that it is said that Martin Luther King, Jr. carried a copy throughout his travels. Over his storied career, Thurman was a founding member of the Congress on Racial Equality (CORE), Professor of Religion at Morehouse and Spelman Colleges, Professor of Religion at Howard University, where he was the first Dean of the Rankin Chapel, co-pastor of the Church for the Fellowship of All Peoples in San Francisco, one of the first intentional interracial churches in the United States, and Dean of Marsh Chapel at Boston University.

Thurman's life spanned the years from Reconstruction and the Great Migration, through the terror of lynching and Jim Crow segregation, through the beginnings of the civil rights movement and the development of active nonviolent resistance, through the upheavals and social revolutions of the 1960s, and into the era of the War on Drugs and the beginning of mass incarceration. All along the way, people interested in what the teachings of Jesus mean for the oppressed have returned again and again to Thurman's work.

While *Jesus and the Disinherited* can be read as an early step in the development of liberation theology, Thurman's work is more accurately read as a "liberating spirituality."[1] In other words, while the implications of Thurman's work for systemic societal change are profound, his text is not only a condemnation of structural injustice but is also a resource for a profound inner resistance grounded in Jesus' message of freedom and love. Thurman's interpretation of the mission of Jesus was born out of his reflection on what the Gospel meant for people "with their backs against the wall."[2] Thurman reflected on the marginalized status of African-Americans, drew from resources in black church traditions, paid attention to anticolonial movements in Africa, met with Gandhi to study creative nonviolent action, and proclaimed the significance of the historical person of Jesus Christ for those who are disinherited.

Thurman's insight into the historical particularity of Jesus as a Jew, from a poor family and a member of an oppressed ethnic group, laid the groundwork for identifying supersessionism[3] as a major issue in the Christian tradition. Thurman recognized that to separate the religion of Jesus from the Jewishness of

---

1   Howard Thurman, Foreword to *Jesus and the Disinherited*.

2   Ibid., 11.

3   Supersessionism – the belief that the Gentile church has replaced Israel as the people of God

Jesus enabled what we now call white supremacy.
By focusing on Jesus' message as arising from
marginalization rather than picturing Christian
mission as directed to the marginalized, Thurman's
work also resists objectifying people in poverty.
The importance of Thurman's work for ministry at
the margins cannot be overstated.

Text

Jesus and the Disinherited

Many and varied are the interpretations dealing with the
teachings and the life of Jesus of Nazareth. But few of these
interpretations deal with what the teachings and the life of
Jesus have to say to those who stand, at a moment in human
history, with their backs against the wall.

To those who need profound succor and strength to enable
them to live in the present with dignity and creativity,
Christianity often has been sterile and of little avail. The
conventional Christian word is muffled, confused, and
vague. Too often the price exacted by society for security
and respectability is that the Christian movement in its
formal expression must be on the side of the strong against
the weak. This is a matter of tremendous significance, for
it reveals to what extent a religion that was born of a people
acquainted with persecution and suffering has become
the cornerstone of a civilization and of nations whose very
position in modem life has too often been secured by
a ruthless use of power applied to weak and defenseless
peoples.

It is not a singular thing to hear a sermon that defines
what should be the attitude of the Christian toward people
who are less fortunate than himself. Again and again

our missionary appeal is on the basis of the Christian responsibility to the needy, the ignorant, and the so-called backward peoples of the earth. There is a certain grandeur and nobility in administering to another's need out of one's fullness and plenty. One could be selfish, using his possessions—material or spiritual—for strictly private or personal ends. It is certainly to the glory of Christianity that it has been most insistent on the point of responsibility to others whose only claim upon one is the height and depth of their need. This impulse at the heart of Christianity is the human will to share with others what one has found meaningful to oneself elevated to the height of a moral imperative. But there is a lurking danger in this very emphasis. It is exceedingly difficult to hold oneself free from a certain contempt for those whose predicament makes moral appeal for defense and succor. It is the sin of pride and arrogance that has tended to vitiate the missionary impulse and to make of it an instrument of self-righteousness on the one hand and racial superiority on the other.

That is one reason why, again and again, there is no basic relationship between the simple practice of brotherhood in the commonplace relations of life and the ethical pretensions of our faith. It has long been a matter of serious moment that for decades we have studied the various peoples of the world and those who live as our neighbors as objects of missionary endeavor and enterprise without being at all willing to treat them either as brothers or as human beings. I say this without rancor, because it is not an issue in which vicious human beings are involved. But it is one of the subtle perils of a religion which calls attention—to the point of overemphasis, sometimes—to one's obligation to administer to human need.

I can count on the fingers of one hand the number of times that I have heard a sermon on the meaning of religion, of Christianity, to the man who stands with his back against the wall. It is urgent that my meaning be crystal clear. The masses of men live with their backs constantly against the wall. They are the poor, the disinherited, the dispossessed. What does our religion say to them? The issue is not what it counsels them to do for others whose need may be greater, but what religion offers to meet their own needs. The search for an answer to this question is perhaps the most important religious quest of modern life.

In the fall of 1935 I was serving as chairman of a delegation sent on a pilgrimage of friendship from the students of America to the students of India, Burma, and Ceylon. It was at a meeting in Ceylon that the whole crucial issue was pointed up to me in a way that I can never forget. At the close of a talk before the Law College, University of Colombo, on civil disabilities under states' rights in the United States, I was invited by the principal to have coffee.

We drank our coffee in silence. After the service had been removed, he said to me, "What are you doing over here? I know what the newspapers say about a pilgrimage of friendship and the rest, but that is not my question. What are you doing over here? This is what I mean.

"More than three hundred years ago your forefathers were taken from the western coast of Africa as slaves. The people who dealt in the slave traffic were Christians. One of your famous Christian hymn writers, Sir John Newton, made his money from the sale of slaves to the New World.

He is the man who wrote 'How Sweet the Name of Jesus Sounds' and 'Amazing Grace'—there may be others, but these are the only ones I know. The name of one of the famous British slave vessels was 'Jesus.'

"The men who bought the slaves were Christians. Christian ministers, quoting the Christian apostle Paul, gave the sanction of religion to the system of slavery. Some seventy years or more ago you were freed by a man who was not a professing Christian, but was rather the spearhead of certain political, social, and economic forces, the significance of which he himself did not understand. During all the period since then you have lived in a Christian nation in which you are segregated, lynched, and burned. Even in the church, I understand, there is segregation. One of my students who went to your country sent me a clipping telling about a Christian church in which the regular Sunday worship was interrupted so that many could join a mob against one of your fellows. When he had been caught and done to death, they came back to resume their worship of their Christian God.

"I am a Hindu. I do not understand. Here you are in my country, standing deep within the Christian faith and tradition. I do not wish to seem rude to you. But, sir, I think you are a traitor to all the darker peoples of the earth. I am wondering what you, an intelligent man, can say in defense of your position."

Our subsequent conversation lasted for more than five hours. The clue to my own discussion with this probing, honest, sympathetic Hindu is found in my interpretation of the meaning of the religion of Jesus. It is a privilege, after so long a time, to set down what seems to me to be

an essentially creative and prognostic interpretation of Jesus as religious subject rather than religious object. It is necessary to examine the religion of Jesus against the background of his own age and people, and to inquire into the content of his teaching with reference to the disinherited and the underprivileged.

We begin with the simple historical fact that Jesus was a Jew. The miracle of the Jewish people is almost as breathtaking as the miracle of Jesus. Is there something unique, some special increment of vitality in the womb of the people out of whose loins he came, that made of him a logical flowering of a long development of racial experience, ethical in quality and Godlike in tone? It is impossible for Jesus to be understood outside of the sense of community which Israel held with God. This does not take anything away from him; rather does it heighten the challenge which his life presents, for such reflection reveals him as the product of the constant working of the creative mind of God upon the life, thought, and character of a race of men. Here is one who was so conditioned and organized within himself that he became a perfect instrument for the embodiment of a set of ideals—ideals of such dramatic potency that they were capable of changing the calendar, rechanneling the thought of the world, and placing a new sense of the rhythm of life in a weary, nerve-snapped civilization.

How different might have been the story of the last two thousand years on this planet grown old from suffering if the link between Jesus and Israel had never been severed! What might have happened if Jesus, so perfect a flower from the brooding spirit of God in the soul of Israel, had been permitted to remain where his roots would have been fed by the distilled elements accumulated from Israel's wrestling with God! The thought is staggering. The Christian Church has tended to overlook its Judaic origins, but the fact is that Jesus of Nazareth was a Jew of Palestine when he went about his Father's business, announcing the acceptable year of the Lord.

Of course it may be argued that the fact that Jesus was a Jew is merely coincidental, that God could have expressed himself as easily and effectively in a Roman. True, but the fact is he did not. And it is with that fact that we must deal.

The second important fact for our consideration is that Jesus was a poor Jew. There is recorded in Luke the account of the dedication of Jesus at the temple: "And when the days of her purification according to the law of Moses were accomplished, they brought him . . . to the Lord; (as it is written in the law of the Lord, Every male that opens the womb shall be called holy to the Lord;) and to offer a sacrifice according to that which is said in the law of the Lord, A pair of turtledoves, or two young pigeons." When we examine the regulation in Leviticus, an interesting fact is revealed: "And when the days of her purifying are fulfilled, for a son, she shall bring a lamb of the first year for a burnt offering, and a young pigeon, or a turtledove, for a sin offering . . . And if she be not able to bring a lamb, then she shall bring two turtles, or two young pigeons; the one for a burnt offering and the other for a sin offering." It is clear from the text that the mother of Jesus was one whose means were not sufficient for a lamb, and who was compelled, therefore, to use doves or young pigeons.

The economic predicament with which he was identified in birth placed him initially with the great mass of men on the earth. The masses of the people are poor. If we dare take the position that in Jesus there was at work some radical destiny, it would be safe to say that in his poverty he was more truly Son of man than he would have been if the incident of family or birth had made him a rich son of Israel. It is not a point to be labored, for again and again men have transcended circumstance of birth and training; but it is an observation not without merit.

The third fact is that Jesus was a member of a minority group in the midst of a larger dominant and controlling group. In 63 B.C. Palestine fell into the hands of the Romans. After this date the gruesome details of loss of status were etched, line by line, in the sensitive soul of Israel, dramatized ever by an increasing desecration of the Holy Land. To be sure, there was Herod, an Israelite, who ruled from 37 to 4 B.C.; but in some ways he was completely apostate. Taxes of all kinds increased, and out of these funds, extracted from the vitals of the people, temples in honor of Emperor Augustus were built within the boundaries of the holy soil. It was a sad and desolate time for the people. Herod became the symbol of shame and humiliation for all of Israel.

In Galilee a certain revolutionary, whose name was Judas, laid siege to the armory at Sepphoris and, with weapons taken there, tried to re-establish the political glory of Israel. How terrible a moment! The whole city of Sepphoris was regarded as a hostage, and Roman soldiers, aided by the warriors of King Aretas of Arabia, reduced the place to whited ash. In time the city was rebuilt—and perhaps Jesus was one of the carpenters employed from Nazareth, which was a neighboring village.

It is utterly fantastic to assume that Jesus grew to manhood untouched by the surging currents of the common life that made up the climate of Palestine. Not only must he have been aware of them; that he was affected by them is a most natural observation. A word of caution is urgent at this point. To place Jesus against the background of his time is by no means sufficient to explain him. Who can explain a spiritual genius—or any kind of genius, for that matter? The historical setting in which Jesus grew up, the psychological mood and temper of the age and of the House of Israel, the economic and social predicament of Jesus' family—all these are important. But they in themselves are unable to tell us precisely the thing that we most want to know: Why does he differ from many others in the same setting? Any explanation of Jesus in terms of psychology, politics, economics, religion, or the like must inevitably explain his contemporaries as well. It may tell why Jesus was a particular kind of Jew, but not why some other Jews were not Jesus. And that is, after all, the most important question, since the thing which makes him most significant is not the way in which he resembled his fellows but the way in which he differed from all the rest of them. Jesus inherited the same traits as countless other Jews of his time; he grew up in the same society; and yet he was Jesus, and the others were not. Uniqueness always escapes us as we undertake an analysis of character.

On the other hand, these considerations should not blind us to the significance of the environmental factors and the social and religious heritage of Jesus in determining the revolutionary character of some of his insights. One of the clearest and simplest statements of the issues here raised, and their bearing upon the character and teaching of Jesus, is found in Vladimir Simkhovitch's *Toward the Understanding of Jesus.* I am using his essay as the basis for our discussion of the problem, but the applications are mine.

Simkhovitch says: "In the year 6 Judea was annexed to Syria; in the year 70 Jerusalem and its temple were destroyed. Between these two dates Jesus preached and was crucified on Golgotha. During all that time the life of the little nation was a terrific drama; its patriotic emotions were aroused to the highest pitch and then still more inflamed by the identification of national politics with a national religion. Is it reasonable to assume that what was going on before Jesus' eyes was a closed book, that the agonizing problems of his people were a matter of indifference to him, that he had given them no consideration, that he was not taking a definite attitude towards the great and all-absorbing problem of the very people whom he taught?"[4]

There is one overmastering problem that the socially and politically disinherited always face: Under what terms is survival possible? In the case of the Jewish people in the Greco-Roman world the problem was even more acute than under ordinary circumstances, because it had to do not only with physical survival in terms of life and limb but also with the actual survival of a culture and a faith. Judaism was a culture, a civilization, and a religion—a total world view in which there was no provision for any form of thoroughgoing dualism. The crucial problem of Judaism was to exist as an isolated, autonomous, cultural, religious, and political unit in the midst of the hostile Hellenic world.

---

4 Pp. 10–11. Copyright 1921, 1937, 1947 by The Macmillan Co. and used with their permission.

If there had been sharp lines distinguishing the culture from the religion, or the religion from political autonomy, a compromise could have been worked out. Because the Jews thought that a basic compromise was possible, they sought political annexation to Syria which would bring them under Roman rule directly and thereby guarantee them, within the framework of Roman policy, religious and cultural autonomy. But this merely aggravated the already tense nationalistic feeling and made a direct, all-out attack against Roman authority inevitable.

In the midst of this psychological climate Jesus began his teaching and his ministry. His words were directed to the House of Israel, a minority within the Greco-Roman world, smarting under the loss of status, freedom, and autonomy, haunted by the dream of the restoration of a lost glory and a former greatness. His message focused on the urgency of a radical change in the inner attitude of the people. He recognized fully that out of the heart are the issues of life and that no external force, however great and overwhelming, can at long last destroy a people if it does not first win the victory of the spirit against them. "To revile because one has been reviled—this is the real evil because it is the evil of the soul itself." Jesus saw this with almighty clarity. Again and again he came back to the inner life of the individual. With increasing insight and startling accuracy he placed his finger on the "inward center" as the crucial arena where the issues would determine the destiny of his people.

When I was a seminary student, I attended one of the great quadrennial conventions of the Student Volunteer Movement. One afternoon some seven hundred of us had a special group meeting, at which a Korean girl was asked to talk to us about her impression of American education. It was an occasion to be remembered. The Korean student was very personable and somewhat diminutive. She came to the edge of the platform and, with what seemed to be obvious emotional strain, she said, "You have asked me to talk with you about my impression of American education. But there is only one thing that a Korean has any right to talk about, and that is freedom from Japan." For about twenty minutes she made an impassioned plea for the freedom of her people, ending her speech with this sentence: "If you see a little American boy and you ask him what he wants, he says, 'I want a penny to put in my bank or to buy a whistle or a piece of candy.' But if you see a little Korean boy and you ask him what he wants, he says, 'I want freedom from Japan.'"

It was this kind of atmosphere that characterized the life of the Jewish community when Jesus was a youth in Palestine. The urgent question was what must be the attitude toward Rome. Was any attitude possible that would be morally tolerable and at the same time preserve a basic self-esteem—without which life could not possibly have any meaning? The question was not academic. It was the most crucial of questions. In essence, Rome was the enemy; Rome symbolized total frustration; Rome was the great barrier to peace of mind. And Rome was everywhere. No Jewish person of the period could deal with the question of his practical life, his vocation, his place in society, until first he had settled deep within himself this critical issue.

This is the position of the disinherited in every age. What must be the attitude toward the rulers, the controllers of political, social, and economic life? This is the question of the Negro in American life. Until he has faced and settled

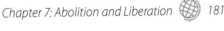

that question, he cannot inform his environment with reference to his own life, whatever may be his preparation or his pretensions.

In the main, there were two alternatives faced by the Jewish minority of which Jesus was a part. Simply stated, these were to resist or not to resist. But each of these alternatives has within it secondary alternatives.

Under the general plan of nonresistance one may take the position of imitation. The aim of such an attitude is to assimilate the culture and the social behavior-pattern of the dominant group. It is the profound capitulation to the powerful, because it means the yielding of oneself to that which, deep within, one recognizes as being unworthy. It makes for a strategic loss of self-respect. The aim is to reduce all outer or external signs of difference to zero, so that there shall be no ostensible cause for active violence or opposition. Under some circumstances it may involve a repudiation of one's heritage, one's customs, one's faith. Accurate imitation until the facade of complete assimilation is securely placed and the antagonism of difference dissolved—such is the function of this secondary alternative within the broader alternative of nonresistance. Herod was an excellent example of this solution.

To some extent this was also the attitude of the Sadducees. They represented the "upper" class. From their number came the high priests, and most of the economic security derived from contemporary worship in the temple was their monopoly. They did not represent the masses of the people. Any disturbance of the established order meant upsetting their position. They loved Israel, but they seem to have loved security more. They made their public peace with Rome and went on about the business of living. They were astute enough to see that their own position could be perpetuated if they stood firmly against all revolutionaries and radicals. Such persons would only stir the people to resist the inevitable, and in the end everything would be lost. Their tragedy was in the fact that they idealized the position of the Roman in the world and suffered the moral fate of the Romans by becoming like them. They saw only two roads open before them—become like the Romans or be destroyed by the Romans. They chose the former.

The other alternative in the nonresistance pattern is to reduce contact with the enemy to a minimum. It is the attitude of cultural isolation in the midst of a rejected culture. Cunning the mood may be—one of bitterness and hatred, but also one of deep, calculating fear. To take up active resistance would be foolhardy, for a thousand reasons. The only way out is to keep one's resentment under rigid control and censorship.

The issue raised by this attitude is always present. The opposition to those who work for social change does not come only from those who are the guarantors of the status quo. Again and again it has been demonstrated that the lines are held by those whose hold on security is sure only as long as the status quo remains intact. The reasons for this are not far to seek. If a man is convinced that he is safe only as long as he uses his power to give others a sense of insecurity, then the measure of their security is in his hands. If security or insecurity is at the mercy of a single individual or group, then control of behavior becomes routine. All imperialism functions in this way. Subject peoples are held under control by this device.

One of the most striking scenes in the movie *Ben Hur* was that in which a Roman legion marches by while hundreds of people stand silently on the roadside. As the last soldier passes, a very dignified, self-possessed Jewish gentleman, with folded arms and eyes smoldering with the utmost contempt, without the slightest shift of his facial muscles spits at the heel of the receding legionary—a consummate touch. Such—in part, at least—was the attitude of the Pharisee. No active resistance against Rome—only a terrible contempt. Obviously such an attitude is a powder keg. One nameless incident may cause to burst into flame the whole gamut of smoldering passion, leaving nothing in its wake but charred corpses, mute reminders of the tragedy of life. Jesus saw this and understood it clearly.

The other major alternative is resistance. It may be argued that even nonresistance is a form of resistance, for it may be regarded as an appositive dimension of resistance. Resistance may be overt action, or it may be merely mental and moral attitudes. For the purposes of our discussion resistance is defined as the physical, overt expression of an inner attitude. Resistance in this sense finds its most dramatic manifestation in force of arms.

Armed resistance is apt to be a tragic last resort in the life of the disinherited. Armed resistance has an appeal because it provides a form of expression, of activity, that releases tension and frees the oppressed from a disintegrating sense of complete impotency and helplessness. "Why can't we do something? Something must be done!" is the recurring cry. By "something" is meant action, direct action, as over against words, subtleties, threats, and innuendos. It is better to die fighting for freedom than to rot away in one's chains, the argument runs.

"Before I'd be a slave I'd be buried in my grave, And go home to my God And be free!"

The longer the mood is contemplated, the more insistent the appeal. It is a form of fanaticism, to be sure, but that may not be a vote against it. In all action there is operative a fringe of irrationality. Once the mood is thoroughly established, any council of caution is interpreted as either compromise or cowardice. The fact that the ruler has available to him the power of the state and complete access to all arms is scarcely considered. Out of the deeps of the heart there swells a great and awful assurance that because the cause is just, it cannot fail. Any failure is regarded as temporary and, to the devoted, as a testing of character.

This was the attitude of the Zealots of Jesus' day. There was added appeal in their position because it called forth from the enemy organized determination and power. It is never to be forgotten that one of the ways by which men measure their own significance is to be found in the amount of power and energy other men must use in order to crush them or hold them back. This is at least one explanation of the fact that even a weak and apparently inconsequential movement becomes formidable under the pressure of great persecution. The persecution becomes a vote of confidence, which becomes, in turn, a source of inspiration, power, and validation. The Zealots knew this. Jesus knew this. It is a matter of more than passing significance that he had a Zealot among his little band of followers, indeed among the twelve chosen ones.

In the face of these alternatives Jesus came forth with still another. On this point Simkhovitch makes a profound contribution to the understanding of the psychology of Jesus. He reminds us that Jesus expressed his alternative in a "brief formula—The Kingdom of Heaven is in us." He states further: "Jesus had to resent deeply the loss of Jewish national independence and the aggression of Rome . . . Natural humiliation was hurting and burning. The balm for that burning humiliation was humility. For humility cannot be humiliated . . . Thus he asked his people to learn from him, 'For I am meek and lowly in heart; and ye shall find rest unto your souls. For my yoke is easy, and my burden is light.'"[5]

It was but natural that such a position would be deeply resented by many of his fellows, who were suffering even as he was. To them it was a complete betrayal to the enemy. It was to them a counsel of acquiescence, if not of despair, full to overflowing with a kind of groveling and stark cowardice. Besides, it seemed like self-deception, like whistling in the dark. All of this would have been quite true if Jesus had stopped there. He did not. He recognized with authentic realism that anyone who permits another to determine the quality of his inner life gives into the hands of the other the keys to his destiny. If a man knows precisely what he can do to you or what epithet he can hurl against you in order to make you lose your temper, your equilibrium, then he can always keep you under subjection. It is a man's reaction to things that determines

---

5   *Toward the Understanding of Jesus*, pp. 60–61. Copyright 1921, 1937, 1947 by The Macmillan Co. and used with their permission.

their ability to exercise power over him. It seems clear that Jesus understood the anatomy of the relationship between his people and the Romans, and he interpreted that relationship against the background of the profoundest ethical insight of his own religious faith as he had found it in the heart of the prophets of Israel.

The solution which Jesus found for himself and for Israel, as they faced the hostility of the Greco-Roman world, becomes the word and the work of redemption for all the cast-down people in every generation and in every age. I mean this quite literally. I do not ignore the theological and metaphysical interpretation of the Christian doctrine of salvation. But the underprivileged everywhere have long since abandoned any hope that this type of salvation deals with the crucial issues by which their days are turned into despair without consolation. The basic fact is that Christianity as it was born in the mind of this Jewish teacher and thinker appears as a technique of survival for the oppressed. That it became, through the intervening years, a religion of the powerful and the dominant, used sometimes as an instrument of oppression, must not tempt us into believing that it was thus in the mind and life of Jesus. "In him was life; and the life was the light of men."

Wherever his spirit appears, the oppressed gather fresh courage; for he announced the good news that fear, hypocrisy, and hatred, the three hounds of hell that track the trail of the disinherited, need have no dominion over them.

I belong to a generation that finds very little that is meaningful or intelligent in the teachings of the Church concerning Jesus Christ. It is a generation largely in revolt because of the general impression that Christianity is essentially an other-worldly religion, having as its motto: "Take all the world, but give me Jesus." The desperate opposition to Christianity rests in the fact that it seems, in the last analysis, to be a betrayal of the Negro into the hands of his enemies by focusing his attention upon heaven, forgiveness, love, and the like. It is true that this emphasis is germane to the religion of Jesus, but it has to be put into a context that will show its strength and vitality rather than its weakness and failure. For years it has been a part of my own quest so to understand the religion of Jesus that interest in his way of life could be developed and sustained by intelligent men and women who were at the same time deeply victimized by the Christian Church's betrayal of his faith.

During much of my boyhood I was cared for by my grandmother, who was born a slave and lived until the Civil War on a plantation near Madison, Florida. My regular chore was to do all of the reading for my grandmother—she could neither read nor write. Two or three times a week I read the Bible aloud to her. I was deeply impressed by the fact that she was most particular about the choice of Scripture. For instance, I might read many of the more devotional Psalms, some of Isaiah, the Gospels again and again. But the Pauline epistles, never—except, at long intervals, the thirteenth chapter of First Corinthians. My curiosity knew no bounds, but we did not question her about anything.

When I was older and was half through college, I chanced to be spending a few days at home near the end of summer vacation. With a feeling of great temerity I asked her one day why it was that she would not let me read any of the Pauline letters. What she told me I shall never forget. "During the days of slavery," she said, "the master's minister would occasionally hold services for the slaves. Old man McGhee was so mean that he would not let a Negro minister preach to his slaves. Always the white minister used as his text something from Paul. At least three or four times a year he used as a text: 'Slaves, be obedient to them that are your masters . . . as unto Christ.' Then he would go on to show how it was God's will that we were slaves and how, if we were good and happy slaves, God would bless us. I promised my Maker that if I ever learned to read and if freedom ever came, I would not read that part of the Bible."

Since that fateful day on the front porch in Florida I have been working on the problem her words presented. A part of the fruits of that search throw an important light upon the issues with which I am dealing. It cannot be denied that too often the weight of the Christian movement has been on the side of the strong and the powerful and against the weak and oppressed—this, despite the gospel. A part of the responsibility seems to me to rest upon a peculiar twist in the psychology of Paul, whose wide and universal concern certainly included all men, bond and free.

Let us examine the facts. The apostle Paul was a Jew. He was the first great creative interpreter of Christianity. His letters are older than the Gospels themselves. It seems that because he was not one of the original disciples, he was never quite accepted by them as one able to speak with authority concerning the Master. This fact hung very heavily upon the soul of the apostle. He did not ever belong, quite. One of the disciples could always say, "But of course you do not quite understand, because, you see, you were not there when . . .

But the fact remains: Paul was a Jew, even as Jesus was a Jew. By blood, training, background, and religion he belonged to the Jewish minority, about whom we have been speaking. But unlike them, for the most part, he was a free Jew; he was a citizen of Rome. A desert and a sea were placed between his status in the empire and that of his fellow Jews. A very searching dilemma was created by this fact. On the one hand, he belonged to the privileged class. He had the freedom of the empire at his disposal. There were certain citizenship rights which he could claim despite his heritage, faith, and religion. Should he deny himself merely because he was more fortunate than his fellows? To what extent could he accept his rights without feeling a deep sense of guilt and betrayal? He was of a minority but with majority privileges. If a Roman soldier in some prison in Asia Minor was taking advantage of him, he could make an appeal directly to Caesar. There was always available to him a protection guaranteed by the state and respected by the minions of the state. It was like a magic formula always available in emergencies. It is to the credit of the amazing power of Jesus Christ over the life of Paul that there is only one recorded instance in which he used his privilege.

It is quite understandable that his sense of security would influence certain aspects of his philosophy of history. Naturally he would have a regard for the state, for the civil magistrate, unlike that of his fellows, who regarded them as the formal expression of legitimatized intolerance. The stability of Paul's position in the state was guaranteed by the integrity of the state. One is not surprised, then, to hear him tell slaves to obey their masters like Christ, and say all government is ordained of God. (It is not to meet the argument to say that in a sense everything that is, is permitted of God, or that government and rulers are sustained by God as a concession to the frailty of man.)

It would be grossly misleading and inaccurate to say that there are not to be found in the Pauline letters utterances of a deeply different quality—utterances which reveal how his conception transcended all barriers of race and class and condition. But this other side is there, always available to those who wish to use the weight of the Christian message to oppress and humiliate their fellows. The point is that this aspect of Paul's teaching is understandable against the background of his Roman citizenship. It influenced his philosophy of history and resulted in a major frustration that has borne bitter fruit in the history of the movement which he, Paul, did so much to project on the conscience of the human race.

Now Jesus was not a Roman citizen. He was not protected by the normal guarantees of citizenship—that quiet sense of security which comes from knowing that you belong and the general climate of confidence which it inspires. If a Roman soldier pushed Jesus into a ditch, he could not appeal to Caesar; he would be just another Jew in the ditch. Standing always beyond the reach of citizen security, he was perpetually exposed to all the "arrows of outrageous fortune," and there was only a gratuitous refuge—if any— within the state. What stark insecurity! What a breeder of complete civil and moral nihilism and psychic anarchy! Unless one actually lives day by day without a sense of security, he cannot understand what worlds separated Jesus from Paul at this point.

The striking similarity between the social position of
Jesus in Palestine and that of the vast majority of American
Negroes is obvious to anyone who tarries long over the
facts. We are dealing here with conditions that produce
essentially the same psychology. There is meant no
further comparison. It is the similarity of a social climate
at the point of a denial of full citizenship which creates
the problem for creative survival. For the most part, Negroes
assume that there are no basic citizenship rights, no
fundamental protection, guaranteed to them by the state,
because their status as citizens has never been clearly
defined. There has been for them little protection from
the dominant controllers of society and even less protection
from the un-restrained elements within their own group.

The result has been a tendency to be their own protectors,
to bulwark themselves against careless and deliberate
aggression. The Negro has felt, with some justification,
that the peace officer of the community provides no
defense against the offending or offensive white man;
and for an entirely different set of reasons the peace
officer gives no protection against the offending Negro.
Thus the Negro feels that he must be prepared, at a
moment's notice, to protect his own life and take the
consequence therefor. Such a predicament has made
it natural for some of them to use weapons as a defense
and to have recourse to pre-meditated or precipitate
violence.

Living in a climate of deep insecurity, Jesus, faced with
so narrow a margin of civil guarantees, had to find some
other basis upon which to establish a sense of well-being.
He knew that the goals of religion as he understood them
could never be worked out within the then-established

order. Deep from within that order he projected a dream, the logic of which would give to all the needful security. There would be room for all, and no man would be a threat to his brother. "The kingdom of God is within." "The Spirit of the Lord is upon me, because he has anointed me to preach the gospel to the poor."

The basic principles of his way of life cut straight through to the despair of his fellows and found it groundless. By inference he says, "You must abandon your fear of each other and fear only God. You must not indulge in any deception and dishonesty, even to save your lives. Your words must be Yea—Nay; anything else is evil. Hatred is destructive to hated and hater alike. Love your enemy, that you may be children of your Father who is in heaven."

Discussion Questions

Woolman sees connections between the desire for wealth, unjust uses of land, people being overworked, and people living in poverty. How does Woolman think the economy, warfare, slavery, and poverty are connected? What might Woolman say about how this works in your community?

Why is it important for Thurman that Jesus was a Jew, from a poor family, and from a people under Roman occupation and oppression? What significance do these facts carry for the church today?

How have you experienced either assimilation or segregation in the church rather than reconciliation and justice? How do you maintain faith in Jesus in the midst of injustice, suffering, racism, and economic inequality?

In what ways does Thurman focus on Christian mission *from* the margins rather than *to the* margins? How is this different or similar to Woolman's understanding of Christian mission? Where is God calling you to position yourself?

Are there practices of resistance to which God is calling you? How can the inner strength spoken of by Thurman lead you to creative action rather than passive silence? What practices would Woolman recommend that you engage in or refrain from?

Chapter 8

Holistic Mission

A nonpossessing person should be free of both miserliness and greed; he should say: "What's mine is yours, and what's yours is also yours."

~ Mary of Paris

Mission is faithful to scripture only to the extent to which it is holistic. In other words, it is faithful when it crosses frontiers (not just geographic but also cultural, racial, economic, social, political, etc.) with the intention of transforming human life in all its dimensions.

~ C. René Padilla

MARY OF PARIS (1891–1945)

Background

Maria Skobtsova was a Russian Orthodox nun who ministered among the poor in Paris and died at the hands of the Nazis alongside Jewish prisoners at the Ravensbrück concentration camp. As a child and young woman, she was known as Liza. Before devoting her life to Christ, Liza professed atheism for a time, was involved in radical politics, and experienced two failed marriages and the death of a child. During these seasons and during the political turmoil of the Bolshevik Revolution, she was increasingly drawn to Jesus Christ. She studied theology, briefly served as a mayor, and was increasingly drawn to justice and social work on behalf of her neighbors. She never gave up her fervor for justice but rather understood it within Jesus' call on her life. She and her family were forced to flee to Paris, where she began to see her vocation as caring for humanity and loving her neighbor. Liza began writing and moved to central Paris to be closer to intense human need. She began lecturing and engaged in charity work with immigrants and workers.

The Russian Orthodox bishop in Paris took notice of Liza's work and gave her permission to start a new form of monasticism, free of the convent and fully engaged in the world with the poor and downtrodden. Liza became a nun, taking the name Mary. Living in a vow of poverty and celibacy and with the support of the church, she opened a house that welcomed impoverished refugees and homeless folks. Over the years, it grew to include a chapel, housing for women, families and men, mental health care, hundreds of daily meals for the poor, care for people with disabilities, and care for people in addiction. To support this work, other nuns and priests joined this new monasticism. Eventually, they founded the group Orthodox Action, which supported homes, schools, camps, hospitals, and publishing works around the world.

Mary of Paris strove to combine theological study and charity/justice work in a way that was fully Christian and fully engaged in the struggles of the world. Involved in both prayer and social action, she found her work to be "too far to the left" for church circles and "too church-minded" for the left.[1] When the Nazis invaded France at the beginning of World War II, Mary had the chance to leave Paris for the United States but refused so that she could stay with the people. She clearly saw that many people would be systematically slaughtered by the Nazi regime. Mary claimed that to be a Christian meant to identify with the yellow star and to join with Israel, God's chosen people. The priest in her monastic community began issuing baptismal certificates to Jews to protect them from being arrested by the Gestapo. She and her fellow monastics helped Jews escape Nazi-occupied Paris and were eventually arrested. When confronted by the Gestapo searching for Jews, Mary and others showed them an icon of Mary and a crucifix of Jesus. She and her fellow ministers were loaded on cattle cars and taken to various concentration camps, where they perished. During her imprisonment at Ravensbrück, Mary continued to minister to many in word and deed. She eventually became extremely ill and was sent to the gas chambers. Mary was canonized a saint by the Orthodox Church in 2004.

---

1   *Mother Maria Skobtsova: Essential Writings*, 31.

In this reading, Mary asks what it means to take a monastic vow of nonpossession, both in literal and spiritual terms. Her words are very helpful for those of us living and ministering in under-resourced contexts today. She encourages us to consider what a monasticism in the world might look like as it engages in Christian mission alongside the poor.

Text

The Poor in Spirit

For many people the promise of blessedness for the poor in spirit seems incomprehensible. What they find incomprehensible are the implications of the phrase "poverty of spirit." Certain fanatics think it means the impoverishment of the spirit, its deliverance from all thinking; they come close to affirming the sinfulness of all thinking, of all intellectual life. Others, who refuse to accept such an explanation, are prepared to consider the word "spirit" little short of an interpolation into the authentic Gospel text.

Let us figure out how we must understand this expression.

In the rite of monastic tonsuring, among other vows, the tonsured person makes a vow of nonpossession, that is, of poverty, which can be understood in a materialist way as a renunciation of the accumulation of material riches. The strict fulfillment of this vow would lead to the blessedness of the poor, but such a narrow and materialist interpretation does not uncover the whole meaning of the phrase: "blessed are the poor in spirit."

The vow of nonpossession can and should be expanded to the spiritual domain; the person who makes it should also renounce spiritual possession, which brings him to the spiritual poverty for which blessedness is promised. But what is spiritual nonpossession?

Nonpossession in general is opposed to two vices between which we make little distinction in our everyday life: the vice of miserliness and the vice of greed. Analyzing them, we will see that a miserly person may not be greedy at all, while a greedy one may even be a spendthrift. It is possible to imagine these two vices in the form of a formula like this. The miserly person says: "What's mine is mine," but does not always add: "What's yours is also mine." The greedy person says: "What's yours is mine," but, again, does not always add: "What's mine is also mine." He may be especially anxious to possess what is not his, while not being very careful about what he has. There exists, of course, a level at which greed combines with miserliness, and vice versa. This is when one says: "What's mine is mine, and what's yours is also mine."

A nonpossessing person should be free of both miserliness and greed; he should say: "What's mine is yours, and what's yours is also yours." And it would be too simple to think that this concerns only material goods. Nonpossession, the absence of miserliness and greed, should concern a person's entire inner world. We know that Christ taught us to lay down our soul for our friends. This laying down of the soul, this giving of oneself, is what makes a person poor in spirit. It is the opposite in everyday life; even with the most negative attitude toward material possession, we are used to regarding the spiritual holding back of ourselves as something positive. Whereas it is the most terrible sin, because it is not material but spiritual.

Thus the virtue of nonpossession, spiritually understood, should make a person open to the world and to people. Life outside the Church, and in part a distorted understanding of Christianity, accustom us to hoarding our inner riches, to being eternally curious—that is, greedy with regard to our neighbor's spiritual world. We often hear it said that man should know measure in his love, should limit himself, and that this measure is his self-preservation, his spiritual well-being, his way of salvation.

Christ did not know measure in His love for people. And in this love He reduced His Divinity to the point of incarnation and took upon Himself the suffering of the universe. In this sense His example teaches us not measure in love but the absolute and boundless giving of ourselves, determined by the laying down of our soul for our friends.

Without striving for such giving of oneself, there is no following the path of Christ.

And it is not Christ but the non-Christian ideal that speaks to us of the hoarding of inner and outer riches. We know what this ideal leads to, we know the egoism and egocentrism that reign in the world, we know how people are turned in upon themselves, upon their own well-being, their peace of mind, their various interests. And we know more. People's care for their spiritual peace, their locking themselves away, leads before our eyes to self-poisoning, demoralization, loss of joy; they become unbearable to themselves . . . In a most paradoxical way, they become poor from holding on to themselves, because their eternal self-attention and self-admiration transform them. The poor hold on to their rags and do not know that the only way not only to preserve them but also to make them precious is to give them with joy and love to those who need them.

And why?

These rags are the corruptible riches of the kingdom of this world. By giving them away, by giving himself away entirely, with his whole inner world, laying down his soul, a man becomes poor in spirit, one of the blessed, because his is the Kingdom of Heaven, according to our Savior's promise, because he becomes the owner of the incorruptible and eternal riches of that Kingdom, becomes it at once, here on earth, acquiring the joy of unmeasured, self-giving, and sacrificial love, the lightness and freedom of nonpossession.

*"By giving them away, by giving himself away entirely . . .
a man becomes poor in spirit, one of the blessed."*

Timothy P. Schmalz, "When I Was Hungry and Thirsty"

C. René Padilla (1932–2021)

Background

Born in Quito, Ecuador, C. René Padilla was a Latin American evangelical theologian and missiologist who lived in Buenos Aires, Argentina. Padilla coined the term *integral mission* (often translated as holistic mission) to stress the importance of both evangelism and social justice as key to Christian mission. Padilla earned a PhD in New Testament from the University of Manchester and was a founding member of the Latin American Theological Fellowship. He worked as the International President of Tearfund, the President of the Micah Network, and Executive Director of Ediciones Kairos. Having served in universities across Latin America, Padilla was actively involved in political conversations about religion and social change. From within contexts that produced Catholic liberation theology, Padilla developed an evangelical social theology.

Padilla was a key thinker at the famous 1974 Lausanne Conference on global mission. Along with many other thinkers, church leaders, and activists, Padilla encouraged the evangelical church to recognize the holistic nature of the Gospel of Jesus Christ. In this Lausanne message on holistic mission, Padilla offers a background of the need for such a formulation, a description of such a theology, the biblical framework for this holistic Gospel, and the role of the local church in engaging in integral mission. Padilla follows in the footsteps of the mothers and fathers of the faith as an evangelical father proclaiming a Christian mission that engages both spiritual and social need.

Text

Holistic Mission

There is general consensus among evangelical Christians all over the world that the church is by nature missionary. But what does that mean? How is the mission of the church defined? What is included in mission? Can mission be circumscribed to transcultural missionary efforts for the sake of the planting of churches in "the regions beyond?" Should mission be identified with evangelism being understood as "the proclamation of the historical, biblical Christ as Savior and Lord, with a view to persuading people to come to him personally and so be reconciled to God?"[2] Or should mission be equated with social transformation resulting from God's action in history through human agency, which may or may not include the church, as has often been advocated in ecumenical circles?

No attempt can be made to answer these questions adequately within the confines of this paper. Enough can be said, however, to account for the description of mission as holistic and to illustrate in practical ways this important concept: a concept that has become increasingly accepted among evangelicals, especially in the Two-thirds World, since the International Congress on World Evangelization, held in Lausanne, Switzerland, in 1974.

1. What Is Holistic Mission?

In a way, the adjective *holistic* only intends to correct a one-sided understanding of mission that majors on either

---

2   John Stott, *Christian Mission in the Modern World* (Downers Grove, IL: InterVarsity Press, 1975), 20.

the vertical or the horizontal dimension of mission. The desire to bring both dimensions together in a biblical synthesis was expressed by the late W. A. Visser t'Hooft in an opening speech at the Uppsala Assembly of the World Council of Churches (1968) in the following words:

> I believe that, with regard to the great tensions between the vertical interpretation of the gospel as essentially concerned with God's saving action in the life of individuals, and the horizontal interpretation of it as mainly concerned with human relationships in the world, we must get out of that rather primitive oscillating movement of going from one extreme to the other, which is not worthy of a movement which by its nature seeks to embrace the truth of the gospel in its fullness. A Christianity which has lost its vertical dimension has lost its salt and is not only insipid in itself, but useless for the world. But a Christianity which would use the vertical preoccupation as a means to escape from its responsibility for and in the common life of man is a denial of the incarnation, of God's love for the world manifested in Christ.[3]

The same aspiration for a more comprehensive view of mission . . . grew consistently throughout the years to such an extent that by the time of the Lausanne Congress, the statement could be made in paragraph 5 of the *Lausanne Covenant* that

> Although reconciliation with man is not reconciliation with God, nor is social action evangelism, nor is political liberation salvation, nevertheless we affirm that evangelism and socio-political involvement are both part of our Christian duty. For both are necessary expressions of our doctrines of God and man, our love for our neighbor and our obedience to Jesus Christ.

---

3   Norman Goodall, ed., *The Uppsala 68 Report* (Geneva: WCC, 1968), 317–18.

> The message of salvation implies also a message of
> judgment upon every form of alienation, oppression and
> discrimination, and we should not be afraid to denounce
> evil and injustice wherever they exist. When people receive
> Christ they are born again into his kingdom and must seek
> not only to exhibit but also to spread his righteousness in
> the midst of the unrighteous world. The salvation we claim
> should be transforming us in the totality of our personal
> and social responsibilities. Faith without works is dead.[4]

Such a statement makes clear that, as Rodger C. Bassham
has pointed out, the Lausanne Congress "produced some
marked changes in evangelical mission theology. . . . through
broadening the focus of the Congress from evangelism to
mission."[5] These "marked changes in evangelical mission
theology" are well illustrated by the "change of mind" that
the well-known British writer and speaker John Stott
experienced between the Berlin Congress (1966) and the
Lausanne Congress. In his opening address on "The
Biblical Basis of Evangelism"[6] at the memorable 1974
Congress, the well-known British author claimed that
"the mission of the church arises from the mission of God"
and should, therefore, follow the incarnational model of
Jesus Christ.[7] On that basis he argued that "mission . . .
describes everything the church is sent into the world to
do," as those who are sent by Jesus Christ even as the Son
was sent by the Father, that is, "to identify with others as

---

4   Stott, *Christian Mission in the Modern World*, 24.

5   Roger C. Bassham, *Mission Theology: 1948–1975 Years of Worldwide Creative Tension: Ecumenical, Evangelical, and Roman Catholic* (Pasadena, CA: William Carey Library), 231.

6   J. D. Douglas, ed., *Let the Earth Hear His Voice: International Congress on World Evangelization, Lausanne, Switzerland* (Minneapolis, MN: World Wide Publications, 1975), 65–78.

7   Ibid., 66–67.

he identified with us" and to serve as "He gave himself in selfless service for others."[8] In his expanded version of the Lausanne address published in 1975 under the title *Christian Mission in the Modern World*, Stott candidly confessed that at the 1966 Congress he had sided with the many who, from the emphasis that most versions of the Great Commission give to evangelism, deduce that "the mission of the church . . . is exclusively a preaching, converting and teaching mission." Then he added:

> Today, however, I would express myself differently. It is not just that the commission includes the duty to teach converts everything Jesus had previously commanded (Matt 28:20), and that social responsibility is among the things which Jesus commanded. I now see more clearly that not only the consequences of the commission but the actual commission itself must be understood to include social as well as evangelistic responsibility, unless we are to be guilty of distorting the words of Jesus.[9]

The affirmation that "the actual commission itself must be understood to include social as well as evangelistic responsibility" seems to suggest a real integration of the vertical and the horizontal dimensions of mission, which is at the very heart of holistic mission . . . The holistic approach was forcefully expressed by the so-called Radical Discipleship group, an ad hoc[10] group of about four hundred participants who met spontaneously during the Congress. Their document on "Theological Implications of Radical Discipleship,"[11] which may be

---

8   Ibid.

9   Stott, *Christian Mission in the Modern World*, 23.

10   Ad hoc – when necessary or as needed

11   Douglas, *Let the Earth Hear His Voice*, 1294–96.

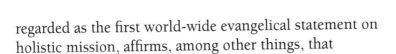

regarded as the first world-wide evangelical statement on holistic mission, affirms, among other things, that

> There is no biblical dichotomy between the Word spoken and the Word made flesh in the lives of God's people. Men will look as they listen and what they see must be at one with what they hear. The Christian community must chatter, discuss and proclaim the gospel; it must express the gospel in its life as the new society, in its sacrificial service of others as a genuine expression of God's love, in its prophetic exposing and opposing of all demonic forces that deny the Lordship of Christ and keep men less than human; in its pursuit of real justice for all men; in its responsible and caring trusteeship of God's creation and its resources.[12]

This definition of holistic mission as including what the church is, what the church does, and what the church says can hardly be improved. The atmosphere generated by the Lausanne Congress has been described as "euphoric," particularly for relief and development workers who "could now appeal to the evangelical constituency as family, without the fear of either being rebuked for preaching the 'social gospel' or being charged of compromising on evangelism."[13] It must be said, however, that after the Lausanne Congress the holistic approach to mission was very much under pressure in conservative evangelical circles. Thus, for instance, the Consultation on World Evangelization (COWE), held in Pattaya, Thailand, in 1980, under the sponsorship of the Lausanne Committee on World Evangelization (LCWE), led many observers to ask how seriously the organizers had taken the

---

12 Ibid., 1294.

13 Vinay Samuel and Chris Sugden, eds., *The Church in Response to Human Need* (Grand Rapids, MI: Wm. B. Eerdmans), ix.

statement made in the *Lausanne Covenant* on the importance of both evangelism and social responsibility. Their concern was voiced by Waldron Scott in the following terms:

> It seems unlikely . . . that the Lausanne Committee will be a major force in the 1980s for promoting a style of evangelism based on a holistic theology and a clear-sighted vision of the definitive contextual realities of the decade. Within evangelical circles we will have to look to groups other than LCWE for leadership along these lines.[14]

2. The Biblical Basis for Holistic Mission

For a proper integration of the various constituent elements of the mission of the church at least three approaches are possible. These three approaches differ only in their focus and are really different parts of one picture.

The first approach takes as its starting point the purpose of God, which embraces the whole of creation. The biblical message of salvation points towards "new heavens and a new earth" and that means that we cannot view salvation as separated from creation. The purpose of salvation is not merely endless life of individual souls in heaven but the transformation of the totality of creation, including humankind, to the glory of God. A person's conversion to Christ is the eruption of the new creation into this world: it transforms the person, in anticipation of the end time, in a wonderful display of God's eschatological purpose to make all things new.

---

14 Quoted by Orlando E. Costas, *Christ Outside the Gate: Mission Beyond Christendom* (Maryknoll, NY: Orbis Books), 154.

This way of looking at conversion has important consequences for evangelism. The purpose of the proclamation of the good news of Jesus Christ is not to change people into religious individuals who cut themselves off from the world in order to enjoy the benefits of their salvation. Rather, the purpose of evangelism is to constitute communities that confess Jesus Christ as the Lord of the totality of life and live in the light of that confession; communities that do not only talk about God's love but also demonstrate it in concrete terms, through good works which God prepared in advance for them to do (Eph 2:10).

The reduction of the Christian mission to the oral communication of a message of otherworldly salvation grows out of a misunderstanding of God's purpose and of the nature of human beings. It is assumed that God wants to "save souls" rather than "to reconcile to himself all things, whether things on earth or things in heaven" (Col 1:20) and that the human being only needs to be reconciled to God rather than to experience fullness of life. In the final analysis, this is a reduction related to ideas taken from Greek philosophy, not from scripture.

Mission is faithful to scripture only to the extent to which it is holistic. In other words, it is faithful when it crosses frontiers (not just geographic but also cultural, racial, economic, social, political, etc.) with the intention of transforming human life in all its dimensions, according to God's purpose and of enabling human beings to enjoy the abundant life that God wants to give to them and that Jesus Christ came to share with them. The mission of the church is multifaceted because it depends on the mission of God, which includes the whole of creation and the totality of human life.

The second approach takes into account that the human being is a unity of body, soul and spirit, which are inseparable. This view, which is taken for granted in both the Old and the New Testament, has been confirmed by modern science. Because the human being is a unity, one cannot properly help a person by taking care of his or her needs of one type (for instance, the need of God's forgiveness, a spiritual need) while disregarding his or her needs of another type (for instance, the material or bodily needs). James acknowledges this when he writes: "Suppose your brother or sister is without clothes and daily food. If one of you says to him, Go, I wish you well; keep warm and well fed, but does nothing about his physical needs, what good is it? In the same way, faith by itself, if it is not accompanied by action, is dead" (James 2:15–17).

From this perspective, holistic mission is mission oriented towards the satisfaction of basic human needs, including the need of God, but also the need of food, love, housing, clothes, physical and mental health and a sense of human dignity. Furthermore, this approach takes into account that people are spiritual, social and bodily beings, made to live in relationship with God, with their neighbors and with God's creation. Consequently, it presupposes that it is not enough to take care of the spiritual wellbeing of an individual without any regard for his or her personal relationships and position in society and in the world. As Jesus saw it, love for God is inseparable from love for neighbor (Matt 22:40). To talk about "holistic mission," therefore, is to talk about mission oriented towards the formation of God-fearing persons who see themselves as stewards of creation and do not live for themselves but for others; persons who are willing to fulfil their God-given vocation in the world and to receive and to give love; persons who "hunger and thirst for justice" and who are "peacemakers" (Matt 5:6, 9).

The third approach to show the integration of the various elements involved in the mission of the church is the one that takes as its starting point the "Christ-Event," including Christ's life and ministry, his death on the cross, his resurrection and his exaltation. Each of these events points towards integral mission as the means whereby the church continues Jesus' mission throughout history and whereby the redemptive work of Jesus takes effect under present circumstances. Since the Lord Jesus Christ is at the heart of God's ultimate purpose for all creation including human beings, focusing on his significance in its fullness will inevitably include the first two approaches, and any other approach, to holistic mission.

3. The Life and Ministry of Jesus and Holistic Mission

The traditional tendency to separate the death of Jesus from his earthly life in order to give prominence to the cross has resulted in a sad lack of attention to the significance of his life and ministry for the mission of the church. Although it is true that the four Gospels emphasize the passion and death of Jesus, it is also true that what gives validity to the death of Jesus Christ as "the atoning sacrifice for our sins" (1 John 4:10) is that it was the sacrifice of the perfect man, whose way of life established the foundations for the definition of what it means to love God above all things and to love one's neighbor as oneself. His earthly life and ministry in this way came to be the model for the life and mission of the church. If that is the case, the proclamation of good news to the poor, the preaching of freedom for captives, of the recovery of sight for the blind and the liberation of the oppressed is a basic criterion by which to assess how far the mission of today's church was really the continuation of the mission of Jesus of Nazareth. As John Perkins says, the church is called to be "the replacement of Jesus in a given community, doing what he would do, going where he would go and teaching what he would teach."

4. *Jesus' Cross and Holistic Mission*

The cross represents the culmination of Jesus' surrender in submission to the will of God for the redemption of humankind. "He made him to be sin who knew no sin, so that in him we might become the righteousness of God" (2 Cor 5:21). This is at the very heart of the gospel. However, the cross also represents the cost of discipleship and of faithfulness to God's call to take part in bringing to fruition his redemptive purpose. The mission of the church provides the link between the death of Jesus Christ on the cross, on one hand, and the appropriation of the justice of God by faith—justification—on the other. As Paul states, the work of reconciliation contains two closely related aspects: God "reconciled us to himself through Christ, and has given us the ministry of reconciliation: that is, in Christ God was reconciling the world to himself, not counting their trespasses against them, and entrusting the message of reconciliation to us" (2 Cor 5:18–19) . . . The church is not truly the church unless it is, according to Bonhoeffer's description, "the church for others," in which the image of "the man for others"—the man who "came not to be served but to

serve and give his life a ransom for many" (Mark 10:45)—
is reproduced . . .

The cross was also the means whereby, according to
Paul, Christ broke down the wall of separation between
Jew and Gentile, thus producing a new humanity, one
body (Eph 2:14–16). The church therefore is called to
demonstrate, both in its life and in its message, this
reconciliation with God and between individuals and
groups. Among those who gather beneath the shadow
of the cross of Christ, oppression that has come to be
associated with ethnic, social and gender divisions
disappear so that "there is no longer Jew or Greek, slave
or free, male or female," but "all of you are one in
Christ Jesus" (Gal 3:28). The church provides a glimpse
of a new humanity that in anticipation incarnates God's
plan, that plan which will be brought to fruition in
"the fullness of time," "to gather up all things, things
in heaven and things on earth" in Christ (Eph 1:10).

5. The Resurrection of Jesus and Holistic Mission

The fulfilment of God's plan for the life and mission of
the church relies on one incomparable resource, the power
with which God raised Jesus from the dead, the power of
the resurrection. No wonder, then, that Paul in his prayer
for the faithful asks God that they might experience the
"immeasurable greatness" of that power (Eph 1:19–20).
The resurrection of Christ is the dawn of a new day in
the history of salvation. It was the confirmation that his
sacrifice had succeeded in overcoming the fatal consequence
of sin, which is death. For those who put their trust in
him, therefore, death does not have the last word. Because
death has been vanquished, Christian hope in the final

victory of God's plan is based on a solid foundation. The
risen Christ is the first fruits of the great harvest, a new
humanity. By His resurrection he has introduced into history
a principle of life which guarantees not only the survival
of the soul for all eternity, but also the permanent validation
of all that the church does through the power of the Spirit
for the cause of Jesus Christ, that is, the cause of love and
justice. The cause of Jesus Christ is the only cause that
has a future. So it makes sense to pray, "Your kingdom
come, your will be done on earth as it is in heaven" and
to strive that the power of the resurrection may become
manifest in the here and now and in every sphere of
human life, and in the whole of creation.

6. The Exaltation of Jesus and Holistic Mission

. . . "It is not for you to know the times or periods that
the Father has set by his own authority. But you will
receive power when the Holy Spirit has come upon you;
and you will be my witnesses in Jerusalem, in all Judea
and Samaria, and to the ends of the earth" (vv. 7–8). The
following comments are relevant.

First, according to Luke these are Jesus' final words
before his ascension. They include the fifth account of
the "Great Commission," in which the missiology of
the whole book of Acts is summarized in narrative form.
Beginning in Jerusalem, the gospel spreads first to the
adjacent areas, Judea and Samaria and then progresses
until it arrives in Rome. In the whole process, the church
occupies a vital place, but not the church alone: it is the
church in the power of the Spirit. The mission is no mere
human project. It is the result of Jesus' mission being
extended in history, an extension made possible by the

action of the Holy Spirit. As such it is brought to fruition, not only by what the witnesses to Jesus say, but also by what they are and do.

Second, Pentecost follows immediately upon the ascension and is inseparable from it. Jesus Christ is enthroned as "Lord and Messiah" (Acts 2:36), King of the universe and from this position sends his Holy Spirit to equip the church for the purpose of making disciples of all nations. The universal horizons of the mission are foreshadowed by the presence in Jerusalem of "devout Jews from every nation under heaven" (v. 5) on the day of Pentecost. The risen Christ, to whom the Spirit bears witness, has been anointed to reign and put his enemies under his feet . . . With the exaltation of Jesus Christ and the coming of the Holy Spirit at Pentecost, a new era has been inaugurated in salvation history: the era of the Spirit, which is at the same time the era of Jesus Christ exalted as Lord and Messiah, and the era of the church and her mission to make disciples in the power of the Spirit.

Third, Jesus' promise to his apostles that he would be with them always, to the end of the age" (Matt 28:20), a promise which accompanied his commission to make disciples of all nations, is fulfilled through the presence of the Spirit and the Word, the combination that made possible the existence of the church and the success of her mission.

Finally, Acts 2:41–47 clearly shows that the result of the Pentecost experience is [not a church] devoted to cultivating individualistic religion and an exclusive, separatist church. On the contrary, it is a community of the Spirit . . . because it incarnates the values of the Kingdom of God and affirms, by what it is, by what it does and by what it says, that Jesus Christ has been exalted as Lord over every aspect of life. It is a missionary community that preaches reconciliation with God and the restoration of all creation by the power of the Spirit. It is a community which provides a glimpse of the birth of a new humanity, and in which can be seen, albeit "in a mirror, dimly" (1 Cor 13:12), the fulfilment of God's plan for all humankind.

7. Historical Perspective on Holistic Mission

. . . The great influence that evangelical Christianity exercised on the social life in the United States during the eighteenth and the nineteenth century has been carefully studied. Many of the social benefits that people enjoy in many countries today, oftentimes without even knowing about their origin, such as the abolition of slavery, labor reforms and all kinds of philanthropic work are part of the legacy of these revivals.

8. The Role of the Local Church

An important deficiency in evangelical theology has been in the area of ecclesiology. For Roman Catholics the church constitutes one of the fundamental theological issues, whereas for evangelicals it tends to be a secondary question. It is hard to calculate the consequences of this lamentable deficiency. The least one can say is that, when the church lacks an ecclesiology rooted in biblical revelation, what takes priority is the institutional church, regulated by human traditions and preoccupied with the achievement of secondary objectives such as its *quantitative* growth, to the detriment of its *qualitative* growth.

Quite definitely, the lack of an adequate ecclesiology has practical consequences related to the way the local church perceives its mission. If mission is not holistic or if mission is seen as a peripheral matter, the minimal condition for the church to fulfil its purpose is missing and the church becomes a religious club with no positive impact on its neighborhood. As the *Micah Declaration on Integral Mission* puts it,

> God by his grace has given local churches the task of integral mission [proclaiming and demonstrating the gospel]. The future of integral mission is in planting and enabling local churches to transform the communities of which they are part. Churches as caring and inclusive communities are at the heart of what it means to do integral mission.

The meaning of "caring and inclusive communities" needs to be spelled out in practical terms if the church is going to be recognized in its own neighborhood as more than a religious institution concerned above all for its own self-preservation. All too often, the stumbling block and the foolishness that prevent non-Christians from turning to Christ is not really the stumbling block and the foolishness of the gospel centered in "Christ crucified" (1 Cor 1:23), but the self-righteous attitude and the indifference to basic human needs on the part of Christians. The first condition for the church to break down the barriers with its neighborhood is to engage with it, without ulterior motives, in the search for solutions to felt needs. Such an engagement requires a humble recognition that the reality that counts for the large majority of people is not the reality of the Kingdom of God but the reality of daily-life problems that make them feel powerless, helpless, and terribly vulnerable.

If that is the case, a top priority for the church that cares is to enable people to articulate their needs, to analyze them, and to reflect on them. Inquiring about what people would like to see changed, what major needs they see in their area, what services they use and what services they lack, and so on, can prevent the church from jumping in with its own agenda. It can also help the church to begin developing meaningful links with the community.

The knowledge of the community based on serious conversation with the people who participate in it is the starting point for the kind of action that is needed—the action that goes beyond paternalistic poverty-relief and helps people to help themselves. Without this kind of empowerment, there is no solution to the problem that underlies many of the problems that affect people, especially the poor, namely, the lack of sense of human dignity oftentimes expressed in terms of marred identities and distorted vocations. Each church is called to be a transformation center that enables people to change their self-perception by seeing themselves as human beings created in the image of God and called to participate in the accomplishment of God's purpose.

Discussion Questions

 Mary pictures a new monasticism lived in the world rather than in a monastery as envisioned by Benedict. How might your faith community live out monastic ideals in your city or community?

 Why would Padilla say that holistic mission corrects a one-sided view of mission? What does it mean that the Word is proclaimed and that the Word is made flesh? How does the Gospel address both spiritual and physical needs? Where do you see the holistic Gospel in Scripture?

 Mary talks about "spiritual nonpossession." How does she distinguish this from "impoverishment of spirit"? In what ways is your heart spiritually or literally greedy? How might your spirit be impoverished?

 Dream about how your faith community could live out a Gospel of both word and deed. Are there holistic ministries or actions God is calling you or your local worshipping community to engage in?

 What disciplines is God calling your faith community to practice so that you can be a part of God's holistic mission in the world?

Afterword

GLOBAL MISSION

Afterword

Now that we have sat down with mothers and fathers of the faith to talk about money and poverty, we have a broader view of Christian mission among the poor. We see that the Gospel of Jesus Christ not only saves souls but also affects people's physical situations. The Gospel doesn't just change hearts; it changes society. The message of Jesus brings both personal spiritual freedom and liberation from bondage.

There are many lessons to be learned from the thinkers in this volume. I'd like to draw your attention to three main points: the Gospel is holistic; the Gospel includes justice and charity; the Gospel brings simplicity and trust.

The Gospel Is Holistic

The word *gospel* means *good news*. The good news of Jesus' incarnation, death, burial, resurrection, and return is that God is reconciling all creation to himself (Col 1:20). God's plan for creation (Gen 1; 2) is restored in the New Creation (Rev 21; 22). In the in-between times that we live in now, Jesus teaches us to pray that God's kingdom would come and God's will would be done on earth as it is in heaven (Matt 6:10). Jesus came that humanity might have abundant life, both now and in the world to come (John 10:10). This does not mean that we should expect prosperity and riches but that the Lord meets the physical needs of those who seek first his kingdom (Matt 6:33). As the body of Christ, when we work to meet the physical needs of others (hunger, thirst, housing, clothing, health, freedom from bondage) we minister to Christ himself (Matt 25:40).

As we engage in God's mission in the world, we are called to love our neighbor as ourselves (Matt 22:39). This means that we desire that our neighbors, especially those who are poor, might have access to the same healthy and whole life we desire for ourselves. We are to love in "deed and in truth," not just "word or talk." (1 John 3:18). "But if anyone has the world's goods and sees his brother in need, yet closes his heart against him, how does God's love abide in him?" (1 John 3:17, ESV).

C. Rene Padilla used the term *holistic* to describe the Gospel. He contended that we must not reduce the Gospel to a message of either spiritual or material salvation alone. The good news includes both! In many ways, this message repeats what the earliest Christians believed. In the *Didache*, we heard Jewish followers of Jesus exhorting us to both personal faithfulness and communal care. The *Didache* called us to share with those in need, refusing to call things our own.

Benedict envisioned communities shaped by worship and work. He saw that the Gospel meant spiritual union with

God and physical care for one another. He understood that, in addition to shaping our lives around prayer, Christians must be committed to limiting the accumulation of wealth and not hoarding things as our own. Mary of Paris demonstrated how these lessons can be lived out not just in the monastery but in our cities and communities. She called Christians to reject miserliness and greed and instead live into postures of spiritual nonpossession, particularly among the poor.

Thomas Aquinas showed us that Christians have always agreed that the Bible doesn't just teach us how to live as individuals but also teaches us how to live in relationship with others, especially those who are poor. He demonstrated that the Gospel affects how we think about property ownership, distribution of resources, and economic systems of lending, debt, and interest. In this sense, the Gospel has political ramifications because it affects the polis, the systems and structures of human community. While the church must not align with a particular political party, nation, or governmental leader, we must live out the holistic Gospel in both personal and social holiness.

The Gospel Includes Justice and Charity

As we have talked with mothers and fathers of the faith, we have seen that the Gospel calls us to alleviate poverty and to care for the poor. Today, Christians often have differing perspectives about whether this means we should provide charity or should work for economic justice. We have seen in these readings that the Christian tradition calls us to both charity and justice.

Basil and Chrysostom stressed the importance of charity for those in need. At the same time, they contended that

Christians should not think that giving to the poor is enough. Rather, it is important that we resist making money in unjust ways, refuse living opulent lifestyles at others' expense, and commit to paying workers their just wages. Basil and Chrysostom saw that how we order our lives together and how we participate in economic systems (justice) are just as important as how we give money away (charity).

John Woolman directed our attention to the ways in which accumulating wealth contributes to misusing land, overworking people, and consigning others to poverty. He saw that the Gospel calls Christians both to give out of our excess (charity) and to consider why it is that some have so much excess to begin with (justice).

Howard Thurman took this insight a step further by stressing that because Jesus was poor and dispossessed, we should see the Gospel as a message *from* the poor and not just *to* the poor. Thurman stressed the inner strength the Gospel brings for the marginalized to resist both assimilation and oppression. Thurman saw the Gospel as a call for justice arising from the poor more than a movement of charity initiated from the wealthy.

The Gospel Brings Simplicity and Trust

As we have conversed with Christian leaders from ages past, we have been called to consider how our inner desires and dispositions toward money and goods affect the way we live. If we worry about our needs being met rather than trusting the God who provides, we are likely to miss what God is doing among the poor.

Clare and Catherine both saw the ways that some people's love of money contributed to other people living in poverty. They also saw that a good way to be free from serving wealth is to desire poverty as holy. While we should not romanticize the kind of poverty that crushes people's spirits and bodies, we can certainly learn from Clare and Catherine that there is something refining about pursuing simplicity instead of riches.

Clement maintains that having wealth is not necessarily wrong, provided that we do not worship it or put our trust in it. However, he also recognizes the soul-threatening dangers of wealth. He explains that people who are wealthy (which today includes the vast majority of North Americans) must submit themselves to spiritual direction and counsel in regard to their use of money. The point here is that no Christian leader in the tradition, even one offering figurative interpretations of Scripture, thought that the unrestricted pursuit of wealth was a good thing.

Martin Luther helpfully summarized the disposition we should have toward money and physical things. He called us to work in obedience to God while trusting God to provide for our needs. He reminded us that God is the creator and that all our human work is simply collecting God's good gifts. He exhorted us to be faithful in the ways we are able, leaving room for the creative work and provision of God.

Conclusion

The mothers and fathers of the faith have shown us that, while Christians may disagree about the details of how to alleviate poverty, we must agree that the Gospel is good news for the poor. The Christian tradition has much to say about how followers of Jesus make money, spend money, and give money away. Christian mission includes recognizing the prominence of the least and the last in the kingdom.

Many of the political arguments modern Christians have about poverty and money miss the point. None of the Christian leaders we have talked with in this book thinks that either an unlimited free market or forced centralized ownership is a good thing. While they may speak about the role of government, their primary concern is calling the church to be a new community, a new society, a new *polis*, in which the poor are elevated and the marginalized are central.

As you continue to read about, reflect upon, and discuss your sacred roots, may you and your community dream together about how to creatively live out Christian mission in the world. Whether you are called to work toward charity amidst people in need, economic development in under-resourced communities, or justice alongside marginalized people, may you find yourself in the company of the saints who have gone before. As we modern Christians connect with the tradition of our faith, may we say along with our new friends that Christianity is the faith of the poor.

Resources for Application

GLOBAL MISSION

Soul Work and Soul Care:
Loving Our Neighbors with Regular Soul Audits

By Hank Voss

No one presumes to teach an art until he has first carefully studied it. Look how foolish it is for the inexperienced to assume pastoral authority, since the care of souls is the art of arts!

~ Gregory the Great, c. 590

Your leaders ... keep watch over your souls and will give an account for their work.

~ Hebrews 13:17a

Each *Sacred Roots Spiritual Classic* has a "Soul Work and Soul Care" resource to illustrate how Christian leaders across cultures and generations have found a particular spiritual classic helpful in pastoral ministry. "Soul work" includes the *personal* work of watering, weeding, pruning, and fertilizing the garden of one's own soul. In a similar way, "soul care" involves the *pastoral* work of nurturing growth in another's friendship with God. When Jesus discusses "soul work" and "soul care," he often uses metaphors from the medical and agricultural professions. Like a doctor for souls, or a farmer caring for an orchard of fruit trees, congregational leaders who hope to serve as "soul surgeons" can learn much from the wisdom of those who have gone before.

Christian Mission and Poverty: Loving our Neighbors with Regular Audits

Concern for the poor is at the heart of Christian mission. The message proclaimed by the teachers of the church over the last two thousand years is one we need today. As John Bunyan notes in *The Pilgrim's Progress*, Christians often become distracted and enticed by the things of this world. The way of Jesus seems hard, and we leave Christ's path to explore Vanity Fair. Table 1 lists several practices the church has used to keep its focus on the people who are a first priority for Jesus (Luke 4:16–21) and his followers (Gal 2:10). Just as many make an annual physical or financial checkup, so we do well to make regular soul checkups in relation to our love and care for the poor. Table 1 provides a number of spiritual practices useful for conducting a soul or ministry audit in relation to this aspect of Christian mission. Table 2 provides specific guidance for how to identify the poor in your community.

Table 1: Spiritual Practices, Soul Audits, and Participating in Christ's Mission to the Poor

Tool	Notes
Sabbath	*Sabbath is a gift to the poor. Practicing sabbath also provides space in the life of all believers to do the hard and dangerous work of worship. Weekly worship calls us away from the idols of our age and into alignment with the mission of Jesus. Find ways to explore a personal and corporate practice of sabbath in your discipleship community.*

Tool	Notes
Almsgiving in Lent	*Forty Days of Focus: For over fifteen centuries millions of believers have annually prepared for Easter with a forty-day period of fasting, prayer, and special attention to the poor (almsgiving). Consider adopting an increased emphasis on care for the poor each Lent leading up to Easter. Perhaps re-reading* Christian Mission and Poverty *could become part of your annual Lenten discipline? Perhaps money saved from fasting from food can be invested in care for the poor in your community? If not during Lent, when does your community conduct an annual audit of its care for the poor?*
The Tithe	*Tithing is a great place to begin to battle the seduction of the love of money (1 Tim 6:10). An annual audit of one's finances can reveal whether we are truly following Jesus in caring for the poor. We must beware becoming like Judas, who talked about the poor loudly while secretly rejecting Jesus in practice (John 12:1–8). What percentage of your annual budget is spent in care for the poor? If care for the poor is a top priority for Jesus, is it also a top priority for you as reflected in your finances?*

For the Lord your God is God of gods and Lord of lords, the great God, mighty and awesome, who shows no partiality and accepts no bribes. He defends the cause of the *fatherless* and the *widow*, and loves the *foreigner* residing among you, giving them food and clothing.

~ Deuteronomy 10:17–18

Followers of Jesus participate in his proclamation of good news to the poor in word and deed. This participation is especially aimed at embracing widows, orphans, and immigrants with the good news about a God who loves them. Individuals and churches pursuing participation in the mission of Jesus will do well to regularly audit their engagement with the poor in their own community. As we learn to love the poor in our midst we are better prepared to love the poor in increasingly distant places, even to the ends of the earth (Acts 1:8).

Table 2: Missional Practices, Neighborhood Audits, and Participation in Christ's Mission to the Poor

Audit Category	Notes
Care for "Widows"	In both the Old Testament and in the New Testament (1 Tim 5) care for elders, especially for elderly women, is an important aspect of mission. Churches today might include not only the elderly, but also the many single parents who struggle to care for children while living in challenging situations. Where are the elderly in your community? Are there forgotten elders with needs your church could meet? Are there single parents you might come alongside to encourage in some way? Participation in Christ's mission in the world always brings blessings. What blessings might you miss by not participating in these missional opportunities?
Care for "Orphans"	Jesus loves children, and he has taught his followers to love them too. North American society today places a low value on unwanted children. Unwanted orphans in the womb are often killed before they are born. Once born, unwanted children are often placed in unwelcoming homes. Where in your community is there opportunity for you as an individual or as a community of disciples to welcome orphans? How might you work for a more just society that loves and welcomes all children into safe and secure homes?

Audit Category	Notes
Care for "Immigrants"	Jesus was a refugee for part of his life. Throughout biblical times, care for the foreigner or immigrant in the land was a litmus test for the faithfulness of God's people. God's people had once been poorly treated immigrants, and they were constantly reminded in Scripture to never forget this fact and to therefore welcome and care for the stranger in their midst. Where are the immigrants in your community? How might you welcome them into your home, your church, and your community?

To learn more about practical ways to love the poor and the neighbors in your own community and around the globe consider the following resources:

Blomberg, Craig L. *Christians in an Age of Wealth: A Biblical Theology of Stewardship*. Biblical Theology for Life. Grand Rapids: Zondervan, 2013.

Davis, Don. "Our Distinctive: Advancing the Kingdom among the Urban Poor." In *Multiplying Laborers for the Urban Harvest: Shifting the Paradigm for Servant Leadership Education*, 15th ed., 23–29. Wichita, KS: The Urban Ministry Institute, 2013.

———. "Christian Mission and the Poor." In *Foundations for Christian Mission*, 4:175–226. Capstone Curriculum. Wichita, KS: The Urban Ministry Institute, 2005.

———. "Jesus and the Poor." In *Foundations for Christian Mission*, 4:251–56. Capstone Curriculum. Wichita, KS: The Urban Ministry Institute, 2005.

Davis, Don, and Terry Cornett. "Empowering People for Freedom, Wholeness, and Justice." In *Foundations for Christian Mission*, edited by Don Davis, 4:310–39. Capstone Curriculum. Wichita, KS: The Urban Ministry Institute, 2005.

Ellul, Jacques. *On Being Rich and Poor: Christianity in a Time of Economic Globalization*. Translated by Willem Vanderburg. Toronto: University of Toronto Press, 2014.

Marchant, Colin, ed. "Lausanne Occasional Paper 22: Christian Witness to the Urban Poor." Lausanne Committee for World Evangelization, 1980. http://www.lausanne.org/all-documents/lop-22.html.

Voss, Hank. "Poor, Theology of The." In *Encyclopedia of Christianity in the Global South*, edited by Mark A. Lamport and George Thomas Kurian, 651–52. Lanham, MD: Rowman & Littlefield, 2018.

Christian Community Development Association. CCDA provides an annual conference, a regular newsletter, and a wide variety of resources for churches and individuals seeking to love their neighbors well. www.ccda.org.

Continuing the Conversation

Many thanks to the translators and publishers who have allowed me to use these ancient and contemporary texts. For the public domain texts translated in Victorian English, I have updated the pronouns (e.g. "thou" to "you") and changed the verbal forms (e.g. "giveth" to "gives"). I have also updated the writing style in the readings from the *Didache*, Clement, Benedict, and Aquinas as the versions available in the public domain contain outdated wording. The rest of the readings are unchanged from the translation listed except for the rare occasion when I have substituted a word in brackets. I have slightly abridged most readings to keep this reader to a reasonable length. Where abridged, the text contains an ellipsis (. . .). The full version of each reading may be found as listed below.

The *Didache*

Translated by M. B. Riddle, *Ante-Nicene Fathers*, Vol. 7. Edited by Alexander Roberts, James Donaldson, and A. Cleveland Coxe. (Buffalo, NY: Christian Literature Publishing Co., 1886.) Revised and edited for New Advent by Kevin Knight. Public Domain. http://www.newadvent.org/fathers/0714.htm.

Clement of Alexandria: *Who Is the Rich Man Who Is Being Saved?*

Translated by William Wilson, *Ante-Nicene Fathers*, Vol. 2. Edited by Alexander Roberts, James Donaldson, and A. Cleveland Coxe. (Buffalo, NY: Christian Literature Publishing Co., 1885.) Revised and edited for New

Advent by Kevin Knight. Public Domain. http://www.
newadvent.org/fathers/0207.htm.

Benedict's Rule

Translated by Rev. Boniface Verheyen, OSB of St.
Benedict's Abbey, Atchison, Kansas. (The 1949 Edition.)
Electronic edition from Christian Classics Ethereal
Library. Public Domain. https://www.ccel.org/ccel/
benedict/rule.xxxiv.html.

Basil the Great: *Sermon to the Rich*

Translated by Peter Gilbert. The Greek text of Basil's
sermon is found in J. P. Migne's *Patrologia Graeca*, vol. 31,
cols. 277C–304C. Electronic edition from Gilbert's blog.
https://bekkos.wordpress.com/st-basils-sermon-to-the-
rich/. Used by permission of Creative Commons. https://
creativecommons.org/licenses/by-nc-nd/3.0/legalcode.

John Chrysostom: *Second Sermon on Lazarus and the Rich Man*

Transcribed by Roger Pearse, Ipswich, UK, 2006. From
John Chrysostom, Four Discourses, Chiefly on the Parable
of the Rich Man and Lazarus, Discourse 2. (1869), pp.
38–58. Public Domain. http://www.tertullian.org/fathers/
chrysostom_four_discourses_02_discourse2.htm.

Clare of Assisi: *First Letter to Agnes of Prague*

Translated by Joan Mueller, OSF. *Clare of Assisi: The
Letters to Agnes.* (Collegeville: Liturgical Press, 2003),
pp. 2–6. Reprinted by permission of translator.

Catherine of Siena: *The Dialogue*

Excerpts from *Catherine of Siena: The Dialogue* translated and introduced by Suzanne Noffke, Copyright © 1980 by Paulist Press, Inc. Paulist Press, Inc., New York/Mahwah, NJ. Reprinted by permission of Paulist Press, Inc. www. paulistpress.com.

Thomas Aquinas: *The Summa Theologica*

Translated by Fathers of the English Dominican Province, *The Summa Theologiæ of St. Thomas Aquinas.* (Second and Revised Edition, 1920). Public Domain. http://www. newadvent.org/summa/3.htm.

Martin Luther: *Brief Exposition of Psalm 127*

Translated by Walther I. Brandt. *Luther's Works, Volume 45: The Christian in Society II.* (Philadelphia: Fortress Press, 1962), pp. 317–337. Reprinted by permission of Fortress Press.

John Woolman: *A Plea for the Poor*

Edited by Phillips P. Moulton. *The Journal and Major Essays of John Woolman.* (Richmond: Friends United Press, 1971), 238–272. Reprinted by permission of Friends United Press.

Howard Thurman: *Jesus and the Disinherited*

Jesus and the Disinherited by Howard Thurman

Copyright © 1976 Howard Thurman

Reprinted with permission from Beacon Press, Boston, Massachusetts

Mary of Paris: *The Poor in Spirit*

Mary Skobtsova, *Mother Maria Skobtsova: Essential Writings*. (Maryknoll: Orbis Books, 2003), pp. 104–106. Reprinted by permission of Orbis Books.

C. René Padilla: *Holistic Mission*

C. René Padilla, *Lausanne Occasional Paper 33: Holistic Mission*. Produced by the Issue Group on this topic at the 2004 Forum for World Evangelization hosted by the Lausanne Committee for World Evangelization in Pattaya, Thailand, 29 September to 5 October, 2004. Reprinted by permission of author.

Further Reading

There are many other works from throughout the Christian tradition that could have been chosen for this classic. The works included were chosen as representative of the diversity of voices and perspectives found in the Christian faith. Even though the authors have distinct emphases and while they might disagree with each other at times, there is yet a discernible narrative running throughout their thinking on Christian mission and poverty. In other words, these thinkers can sit down at the table together and provide a coherent conversation about how Christians should live in light of issues related to poverty and people who are poor.

If you would like to talk with more mothers and fathers of the faith or current church leaders about Christian mission and poverty (or if you would like to hear more from the ones in this volume), you would do well to consult the following:

Athanasius of Alexandria, *Life of St. Anthony of Egypt*. Translated by H. Ellershaw, *Nicene and Post-Nicene Fathers, Second Series, Vol. 4*. Edited by Philip Schaff and Henry Wace. (Buffalo, NY: Christian Literature Publishing Co., 1892.) Revised and edited for New Advent by Kevin Knight. http://www.newadvent.org/fathers/2811.htm. This classic work is a good introduction to the monastic impulse: the call to leave economic and political centers in pursuit of poverty and faithfulness to Jesus.

Booth, Catherine and William, *Aggressive Christianity: A Passionate Call for Christian Social Justice* (Pantianos Classics, 1880). This work is written by the founders of the Salvation Army and demonstrates their commitment to preaching the Gospel among the poor.

Francis and Clare: The Complete Works. (Mahwah: Paulist Press, 1982). Translation and introduction by Regis J. Armstrong, OFM CAP and Ignatius C. Brady, OFM. This work contains the complete writings of Francis, the "little poor brother" and founder of the Friars Minor, and Clare, the founder of the Poor Sisters.

Oden, Thomas C., *The Good Works Reader* (Grand Rapids, Eerdmans, 2007). This reader presents a thorough sampling of what the mothers and fathers of Christian faith had to say about how Christians should live our lives. This text includes many ancient reflections on Christian mission and poverty.

St Basil the Great, *On Social Justice*. (Crestwood: St Vladimir's Seminary Press, 2009). Translation and introduction by C. Paul Schroeder. This text includes Basil's The Sermon to the Rich and three more of his sermons focused on the themes of Christian mission and poverty.

St John Chrysostom, *On Wealth and Poverty*. (Crestwood: St Vladimir's Seminary Press, 1981). Translation and introduction by Catharine P. Roth. This text includes the entire cycle of Chrysostom's sermons on the rich man and Lazarus.

St Suplitius Serverus, *Saint Martin of Tours*. (Aeterna Press, 2015). This text describes the life of a Roman soldier who became a Christian, gave up warfare, and spent his life in service of the poor.

St. Gregory of Nyssa Ascetical Works. (Washington, D.C.: The Catholic University of America Press, 1967), especially *The Life of St. Macrina*. As a brother of Basil, Gregory of Nyssa represents Cappadocian teaching on the Christian life and poverty. In this text, he shows how their older sister Macrina guided them in pursuing Jesus, theology, poverty, and ministry.

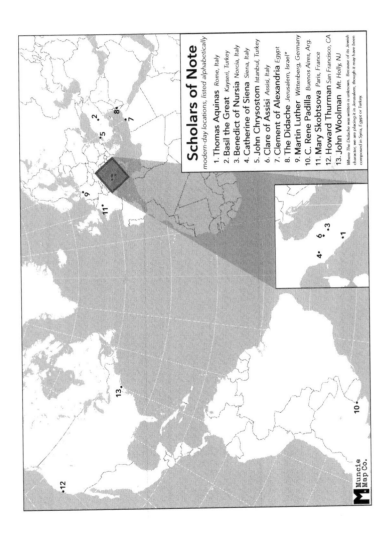

Map of Important Places:
Scholars of Note

Scholars of Note
modern-day locations, listed alphabetically

1. Thomas Aquinas Rome, Italy
2. Basil the Great Kayseri, Turkey
3. Benedict of Nursia Norcia, Italy
4. Catherine of Siena Siena, Italy
5. John Chrysostom Istanbul, Turkey
6. Clare of Assisi Assisi, Italy
7. Clement of Alexandria Egypt
8. The Didache Jerusalem, Israel*
9. Martin Luther Wittenberg, Germany
10. C. Rene Padilla Buenos Aires, Arg.
11. Mary Skobtsova Paris, France
12. Howard Thurman San Francisco, CA
13. John Woolman Mt. Holly, NJ

*Where The Didache was written is unknown. Because of its Jewish character, we are placing it in Jerusalem, though it may have been composed in Syria, Egypt or Turkey.

Muncie Map Co.

A Letter to God's Friends and Fellow Warriors On Why We Read the Sacred Roots Spiritual Classics Together

---

Scholars like big books; small books change the world.

~ Rev. Dr. Glen Scorgie

Dear Friends and Fellow Warriors,

Greetings in the strong name of Jesus! What a joy to know that Jesus calls us "Friend" (John 15). What an honor to stand with sisters and brothers from every century and culture to shout, "Worthy is the Lamb!" What a privilege to serve in the Lamb's army, not fighting flesh and blood, but God's *internal* (the flesh), *external* (the world) and *infernal* (the Devil) enemies. In light of this cosmic struggle, we put on a wartime (not peacetime) mindset as we follow Jesus. Moses stated that God is present and at work in every generation (Ps 90:1), and the *Sacred Roots Spiritual Classics* are for those who desire to be used within their sphere of influence like David was used by God in his generation (Ps 57:2; Acts 13:36).

Our Context: A Battle with God's Internal, External, and Infernal Enemies

Scripture teaches our daily need to choose a missional mindset (Matt 6:10). God's kingdom never advances in neutral territory. Every inch in creation, including each inch of our soul, is a contested battlefield. God's enemies are threefold. First, there is an *internal* enemy hiding within the heart of each redeemed child of God. God

loves us, even though we often battle a "Judas-heart"—
a tendency to betray our Lord (John 12:6). Scripture
names this brokenness the "flesh," the old "man" or the
"sin nature" (Rom 8; Gal 5–6). We work to kill ("mortify")
this sin lest it succeed in killing us (Rom 6:13).

Second, as followers of Jesus, we battle all *external*
enemies opposing the Lamb's kingdom. Sickened by sin,
polluted by greed, corrupted by self-centeredness,
idolatry and oppression; our world is not the way it is
supposed to be. What God created good has been twisted
and now often grieves the Holy Spirit. We choose to
stand with Shadrach, Meshach and Abednego in refusing
to bow to the principalities and powers of the age (Dan
3), or to accept the besetting sins of our ethnicities,
nations and generations. Scripture and our sacred roots
shine painful yet purifying light on our blind spots.

Finally, we are not ignorant of the Devil's schemes. We may
not know if a demon's name is "Screwtape" or "Legion,"
but we do know that an *infernal* enemy opposes God's
kingdom *shalom*. He is the Devil, Satan, the Father of
Lies, the Accuser, and one day soon he and his demons
will be completely crushed. In this time between the
times, the Lamb's followers resist and renounce the Devil
and all his ways with the sword of the Spirit which is the
Word of God.

Our Mission: To Be Faithful Stewards and Wise Servants in Our Generation

Scripture contains a number of "history" psalms (Pss 78,
105, 106, 136; Neh 9:6–38; cf. Heb 11). These songs
challenge us to reflect on women and men who chose to
serve God in their generation—Abraham and Sarah,

Moses, Phinehas, Rahab, David, Esther and many others. History psalms also warn of those who ignored or refused to participate in God's work (Pharaoh, Dathan, Abiram, Og). Leaders like Rahab the prostitute (Matt 1:5; Heb 11:35; James 2:25) and King David were far from perfect (Ps 51). Yet Scripture declares that leaders like David "served the purposes of God in his own generation" (Acts 13:36).

Do you want God to use you in your generation? Are you willing to be a David or Esther today? God is already at work in our communities, schools and workplaces. Sometimes the neighborhoods with the greatest challenges (those with giants like "Goliath" and armies of Philistine enemies) are the very places God finds servants and stewards he can use (1 Sam 17; 1 Cor 4:1).

Like King David, Prince Kaboo of the Kru people in Liberia chose to participate in God's work in his generation. As a child, Prince Kaboo (1873–1893) was taken hostage by a rival tribe and was about to be executed when he experienced a supernatural deliverance. After weeks of traveling through the jungle, Kaboo arrived a mission station near Monrovia, Liberia's capital. There, as a fourteen-year-old teenager, he wholeheartedly gave his life to Jesus Christ.

Prince Kaboo took on the name Samuel Kaboo Morris at his baptism, and he spent the next four years working and studying Scripture—especially Jesus' teaching about the Holy Spirit as recorded by his friend John (John 14–17). Kaboo was fascinated with the Holy Spirit, for he had personally experienced the Holy Spirit's powerful deliverance. Eventually, the missionaries told Kaboo they had taught him all they knew and that if he wanted to learn more about the Holy Spirit, he would need to travel to the United States. Kaboo felt the need for more training about the Holy Spirit before being ready to return to the Kru as an evangelist. With no shoes or money, Kaboo walked to Monrovia's harbor to find passage to New York—trusting his Father in Heaven to provide.

Kaboo's story is powerful. The ship that transported Kaboo experienced revival with the captain and many crew coming to Christ. Within a few hours of arriving in New York, Kaboo led seventeen men to Christ at an inner-city rescue mission. On his third day in the United States, the eighteen-year-old evangelist preached at a Sunday school meeting and revival broke out with a new missionary society organized that very day. God provided money for Kaboo's college tuition, housing, books and necessities. By the end of his first week in America, Kaboo had arrived in Fort Wayne, Indiana to begin studying at Taylor University—an evangelical college committed to raising up workers for the harvest fields who walk in the power of the Holy Spirit (Matt 9:36; Acts 1:8).

Prince Kaboo's arrival at Taylor University transformed not only Taylor University's campus, but also the whole city of Fort Wayne. On his first Sunday in town, Kaboo walked to the front of the church and asked for permission to pray. As he prayed, the power and presence of the Holy

Spirit descended on the congregation in a way none had ever experienced before. The pastor reported, "what I said and what Sammy said I do not remember, but I know my soul was on fire as never before. . . . No such visitation of the Holy Spirit had ever been witnessed" by our congregation.[1]

Two years later, on May 12, 1893, at the age of twenty, Prince Samuel Kaboo Morris died from an illness contracted after traveling through a snowstorm to preach. Since his death, Kaboo's story has influenced thousands of students at Taylor University and elsewhere to participate with the Holy Spirit in mission and seek the Spirit's power in witness. John Wengatz was a student at Taylor in 1906, the year he first read Kaboo's story. Some fifty years later, after a lifetime invested as a missionary in Africa, Wengatz remarked "my tears never cease to flow as I read that unrepeatable story."[2] Although Kaboo died at twenty, he was used mightily by God in his generation. Will those who tell the story of your life say the same?

Our Vision: Toward Ten Thousand "Tozers"

If you are pursuing God with the same passion and hunger displayed by Samuel Kaboo Morris, than you will be glad to meet A. W. Tozer (1897–1963). Tozer grew up poor without the opportunity to complete high school. While working in a tire factory he heard the good news

---

1   Lindley Baldwin, *Samuel Morris: The African Boy God Sent to Prepare an American University for Its Mission to the World* (Minneapolis, MN: Bethany House, 1987), 59.

2   John Wengatz, *Sammy Morris: Spirit-Filled Life* (Upland, IN: Taylor University Press, 1954), Preface.

about Jesus, repented and believed. At nineteen, he began to preach, becoming one of the most influential pastors in his generation. His books *The Pursuit of God* and *The Knowledge of the Holy* have helped millions know and love the Triune God revealed in Scripture. When asked how he learned to read Scripture with such clarity and theological depth, Pastor Tozer would often point to his "friends" and "teachers." These teachers were a list of some thirty-five Christian spiritual classics read and reread throughout Tozer's life. *Sacred Roots Spiritual Classics* (*SRSC*) are for those with a hunger for the Holy Spirit like Prince Kaboo and a desire to be used like Pastor Tozer.

The Sacred Roots Project envisions ten thousand Christian leaders, serving in challenging ministry contexts across North America, engaging with spiritual classics in community by the year 2030. Will you join this growing community as we pursue God together by reading and discussing spiritual classics with gospel friends and kingdom co-workers (Matt 9:35)?

A larger dream also informs the Sacred Roots Project—a dream that imagines a million Christian workers equipped to serve among the global poor (Matt 9:36–38). The Center for the Study of Global Christianity reports that in the middle of 2020 there are approximately two and a half billion people living in urban poverty.[3] This number will increase to over four billion by the year 2050. Sacred Roots dreams of equipping one million Christian leaders among this great multitude—women and men like Prince Kaboo—with access to excellent editions of some of the greatest spiritual classics the Christian tradition has

---

3   For the most current statistics, see www.gordonconwell.edu/center-for-global-christianity/resources/status-of-global-christianity/.

produced. Ultimately, the goal is increased faithfulness as leaders mature in representing Christ in local churches that are centered on Scripture, grounded in Great Tradition truth (Nicene), and engaged in contextually relevant witness to Christ's love in thousands of diverse contexts.[4]

Our Strategy:
Scripture, Friendship and Spiritual Classics

Sacred Roots' strategy is simple. We believe fresh readings of Christian spiritual classics can lead Christian leaders into a deeper engagement with the God revealed in Scripture and into deeper friendships with one another.

Christian spiritual classics strengthen and deepen our roots in Scripture and help us produce the Spirit's fruit. One day Jesus asked a serious student of the Bible a simple question, *"How do you read it?"* (Luke 10:26). Of the more than three hundred questions asked by Jesus in the Gospels, few are more relevant today. Faithfulness in our generation demands that we learn to read Scripture in a way consistent with the foundational truths held by followers of Jesus in every culture since the first century. We read Christian spiritual classics to discover faithful and fruitful readings of Scripture. As Dr. Davis has noted, the church's "Great Tradition" perennially opens our eyes to new riches in Scripture's "Authoritative Tradition."[5]

A truth believed by all Christians, in all places, and at all times is that there is one God who exists as Father, Son, and Holy Spirit. From "before to beyond time," an eternal

---

4   Don Davis, *Sacred Roots: A Primer on Retrieving the Great Tradition* (Wichita, KS: The Urban Ministry Institute, 2010), 35–45.

5   Ibid.

friendship between the Trinity's three persons has existed at the center of reality. Spiritual friendship provides the start and heart of truth. Just as spiritual classics can reveal new riches from Scripture, so they help us grow in love for God and neighbors. They can provide practical help in deepening our friendships with the Father, the Son, the Holy Spirit and with other believers—both with believers in this generation and with those surrounding us in the great cloud of witnesses (Heb 12:1; 13:7). Why do Christian leaders desperately need to pursue strong friendships? Start with these three reasons.

1. First, each of us has eyes far too small to see what God wants to show us! No one can begin to grasp the great things God is doing across 100 billion galaxies and throughout the many generations since the universe's creation. Friends, standing in different places provides additional eyes to see from different perspectives what God is doing in the world and across history.

2. Second, each of us battles a sinful nature that distorts our perception of the truth. We need friends who speak truth to us, sharpening us like iron sharpening iron (Prov 27:17).

3. Third, all of us view creation through a particular culture's time and place. Each culture exists with a unique version of virtue and vice. Friends who speak to us from other cultures and centuries often affirm virtues in our culture, but they can also reflect ways our culture's vice habitually offends against kingdom *shalom*.

In sum, *Sacred Roots Spiritual Classics* help us grow in our friendship with God and neighbor (Matt 22:37–40). Neighbors include the living Christian leaders with whom we read and discuss this spiritual classic. However, "neighbor" also includes the author (or authors) of this spiritual classic. These women and men walked faithfully with God and neighbor. Their life and teachings produced good fruit in their generation and then continued to do so in the lives of other Christian leaders—often across many cultures and centuries. As an editorial team, we can personally testify to the fruitfulness of the time we have spent with our "friends," the "ancient witnesses" in the *Sacred Roots Spiritual Classics*. If you choose to invest in careful conversation with these saints of old (Heb 13:7), we are confident you will not only experience practical fruit in the present, but you will also gain new friends for eternity.

Tactical Notes: Christian Leaders Are Christian Readers

Throughout church history, fruitful Christian leaders have been intentional readers. Augustine (d. 430), a pastor and bishop in Africa, was challenged to a new level of ministry by reading a spiritual biography about an Egyptian Christian leader named Anthony (d. 356).[6] Protestant leaders like Martin Luther, John Calvin, John Wesley, Elizabeth Fry, Phoebe Palmer and many others all published editions of spiritual classics for Christian leaders in their generation. Charles Harrison Mason (d. 1961), founder of the largest Pentecostal denomination in North America (Church of God in Christ), was called to ministry through a reading

---

6   Athanasius, *Renewal in Christ: Athanasius on the Christian Life*, ed. Jeremy Treat, *Sacred Roots Spiritual Classics 6* (Wichita, KS: The Urban Ministry Institute, 2022).

of the autobiography of missionary and evangelist Amanda Smith.[7] More recently, leaders like C. S. Lewis, A. W. Tozer, James Houston, and Rick Warren have encouraged Christian leaders to read wisely, especially choosing Christian spiritual classics.[8]

How to Read the Text

Plan **your reading.** Reading a spiritual classic is a bit like reading your Bible. You can read it anywhere or anytime, but there are times and places that will position you to better receive insight and truth. *SRSC* readers tend to read each spiritual classic several times, and many will "read" it in both a written version (print or electronic) and in an audible version (audio book). We read to hear what the original author of the text is saying and to understand what the Holy Spirit might be directing our attention to hear or reflect upon. On your day of rest (Sabbath) reserve some time to read or at least set aside some time to plan when you will read from your spiritual classic that week. If you have a daily commute, perhaps use some of the time to listen and reflect on an audible version of the *SRSC*.

Work **your reading plan.** Once you have planned to read your spiritual classic, begin with the **Introduction.** The introduction is written by a contemporary friend with significant ministry experience. This friend has spent much

---

7 Amanda Smith, *An Autobiography: The Story of the Lord's Dealings with Mrs. Amanda Smith, the Colored Evangelist; Containing an Account of Her Life Work of Faith, and Her Travels in America, England, Ireland, Scotland, India, and Africa, as an Independent Missionary* (Chicago: Meyer, 1893).

8 Explore the essays in Jamin Goggin and Kyle Strobel, eds., *Reading the Christian Spiritual Classics: A Guide for Evangelicals* (Downers Grove, IL: InterVarsity, 2013).

time reading and getting to know the spiritual classic and the author who wrote it. Often, the introduction is written by someone who has read the spiritual classic dozens, if not hundreds, of times. The introduction will help you get the most out of your first several readings of the text.

After reading the Introduction, notice that all *Sacred Roots Spiritual Classics* are divided into eight **Chapters**. These chapters are not always of equal length, but they all are weighty enough to engage your head, heart, and hands as well as your habitat and habits. Following the eight chapters, every *SRSC* includes a short section called **Continuing the Conversation**. If you enjoyed reading the spiritual classic, then Continuing the Conversation will help you discover more resources to engage the author(s) of the spiritual classic.

The *Sacred Roots Spiritual Classics* are divided into ten parts to make it easier to talk about the text with friends and co-workers. The table below provides four (of many) examples of how to read a *SRSC* with a group of friends. When friends commit to read and discuss a *SRSC* together, the group is called a **Sacred Roots Cohort.**

SRSC Section to Read	"Sunday School" Class	"Church-Based Seminary" Module	Monthly Pastor's Meeting	Quarterly Retreat Discussion Group
	Ten Weeks	*Eight Weeks*	*Monthly*	*Quarterly*
Introduction	Week 1	Week 1	Month 1	Read text before retreat and then discuss
Ch. 1	Week 2	Week 1	Month 1	Read text before retreat and then discuss
Ch. 2	Week 3	Week 2	Month 1	Read text before retreat and then discuss
Ch. 3	Week 4	Week 3	Month 2	Read text before retreat and then discuss
Ch. 4	Week 5	Week 4	Month 2	Read text before retreat and then discuss
Ch. 5	Week 6	Week 5	Month 2	Read text before retreat and then discuss
Ch. 6	Week 7	Week 6	Month 2	Read text before retreat and then discuss
Ch. 7	Week 8	Week 7	Month 3	Read text before retreat and then discuss
Ch. 8	Week 9	Week 8	Month 3	Read text before retreat and then discuss
Continuing the Conversation	Week 10	Week 8	Month 3	Read text before retreat and then discuss

Review **your reading.** The best readers, like the best leaders, do more than make a plan and work it. They also pause to take time to review their work—or in this case—their reading.[9] Robert Clinton has noted that only around 25% of leaders in the Bible finished well.[10] If we hope to finish well in our generation we must learn to *attend* to our habitat, our head, our heart, our hands, and our habits. To *attend* means to pay attention, to apply our self, to prioritize and to value something enough to give it our time and our energy. Each chapter concludes with five types of questions aimed at helping you review your progress toward finishing well and hearing Jesus say, "Well done, good and faithful servant" (Matt 25:23).

Habitat? Habitat questions ask us to pause and look around at our environment, our culture, our generation, our nationality, and the things that make up the *Zeitgeist* (spirit of the times). Questions may ask about the author's habitat or our own. Since the *SRSC* were written across many centuries and cultures, they often help us notice aspects of our culture needing attention.

Head? Auguste Rodin's sculpture known as *The Thinker* sits before an 18-foot-tall sculpture called *The Gates of Hell*. The massive sculptural group reflects Rodin's engagement with a spiritual classic by Dante, *The Divine Comedy*. *Head questions* require serious intellectual

---

9   The PWR (Plan, Work, Review) process is explained further by Don Allsman, *The Heroic Venture: A Parable of Project Leadership* (Wichita, KS: The Urban Ministry Institute, 2006).

10 Robert Clinton, *The Making of a Leader: Recognizing the Lessons and Stages of Leadership Development*, Rev. ed. (Colorado Springs, CO: NavPress, 2012), 185–87.

engagement as you talk with friends about the author's ideas, claims, and proposals.

Heart? In August of 1541 John Calvin wrote a letter to a friend with this promise: "When I remember that I am not my own, I offer up my heart presented as a sacrifice to God." Calvin's personal seal expressed this sincere desire. God not only owns our mind, but also our will and emotions. *Heart questions* will help you attend to the people and things to which you give your loves.

Hands? Albrecht Dürer sketched a drawing called *Study of the Hands of an Apostle* in the year 1508. The apostles were men of action, yet Dürer portrays the apostle's hands in prayer. The action to which *SRSC* call us are often surprising. *Hands questions* will challenge you to evaluate carefully what action you are to take after a particular reading.

Habits? Charlotte Mason (d. 1923) was a master teacher. She believed Christian formation must carefully attend to habit formation. Like laying railroad tracks, habit formation is hard work. But once laid, great work requires little effort just as railroad cars run smoothly on tracks. *Habit questions* challenge you to reflect on small daily or weekly actions that form your character and the character of those around you.

Reading with Friends

The *Sacred Roots Spiritual Classics* are not meant to be read alone; indeed, it is impossible to do so. Every time we open a *SRSC* we read a book that *has been read* by thousands of Christian leaders in previous generations, *is being read* by thousands of Christian leaders in our generation, and *will be read* (if the return of Christ tarries) by thousands of Christian leaders in generations after us. The readers before us have already finished their race. These thousands of Christian leaders read the text in hundreds of different cultures and across dozens of different generations. All these "friends" read this text with you now. As you read the *SRSC*, imagine yourself talking about *Benedict's Rule* (*SRSC 2*) with the reformer Martin Luther; or picture yourself discussing Madam Guyon's *A Short and Easy Method of Prayer* with the missionary Amy Carmichael. Remember you never read a *Sacred Roots Spiritual Classic* alone.

However, it is not just leaders who have gone before, it is also leaders in the present with whom you must imagine reading this *SRSC*. Whatever benefit you find in reading will be doubled when you share it with a friend. Whatever trouble or difficulty you find in reading the text will be halved when you share it with a friend. Resolve to never read a *Sacred Roots Spiritual Classic* alone.

Perhaps you have noticed that the word "generation" has already appeared in this preface more than fifteen times? The *SRSC* represent the work of many generations working together. Five generations of evangelicals have worked and prayed together on this project since its public commencement in 2018. But these five generations of living evangelicals represent only a small sample of the many generations who have tested the faithfulness and fruitfulness of the *SRSC*. Why does this matter? In part, it matters because these texts are treasures to use and then pass on to the next generation of leaders. Recognize the emerging leaders God has called you to serve and steward—share the *Sacred Roots Spiritual Classics* with them.

Careful readers of Scripture know that the most influential leaders among God's people have always worked in teams. King David's teams became legends—"the three," "the thirty." The list of Paul's missionary and ministry team members whose first name we know from the New Testament runs to nearly one hundred. Our Sacred Roots team of teams prays that this text will be a blessing and a reliable resource for you and your gospel friends as you pursue kingdom business together.

Grace and Peace,

Don, Uche, Greg, May, Ryan, Isaiah, and Hank

The Nicene Creed with Scriptural Support

The Urban Ministry Institute

We believe in one God,
> *Deut 6:4–5; Mark 12:29; 1 Cor 8:6*

the Father Almighty,
> *Gen 17:1; Dan 4:35; Matt 6:9; Eph 4:6; Rev 1:8*

Maker of heaven and earth
> *Gen 1:1; Isa 40:28; Rev 10:6*

and of all things visible and invisible.
> *Ps 148; Rom 11:36; Rev 4:11*

We believe in one Lord Jesus Christ, the only Begotten Son of God, begotten of the Father before all ages, God from God, Light from Light, True God from True God, begotten not created, of the same essence as the Father,
> *John 1:1–2; 3:18; 8:58; 14:9–10; 20:28; Col 1:15, 17; Heb 1:3–6*

through whom all things were made.
> *John 1:3; Col 1:16*

Who for us men and for our salvation came down from heaven and was incarnate by the Holy Spirit and the Virgin Mary and became human.
> *Matt 1:20–23; Luke 19:10; John 1:14; 6:38*

Who for us too, was crucified under Pontius Pilate, suffered and was buried.
> *Matt 27:1–2; Mark 15:24–39, 43–47; Acts 13:29; Rom 5:8; Heb 2:10; 13:12*

The third day he rose again according to the Scriptures,
Mark 16:5–7; Luke 24:6–8; Acts 1:3; Rom 6:9; 10:9; 2 Tim 2:8

ascended into heaven, and is seated at the right hand of the Father.
Mark 16:19; Eph 1:19–20

He will come again in glory to judge the living and the dead, and his Kingdom will have no end.
Isa 9:7; Matt 24:30; John 5:22; Acts 1:11; 17:31; Rom 14:9; 2 Cor 5:10; 2 Tim 4:1

We believe in the Holy Spirit, the Lord and life-giver,
Gen 1:1–2; Job 33:4; Pss 104:30; 139:7–8; Luke 4:18–19; John 3:5–6; Acts 1:1–2; 1 Cor 2:11; Rev 3:22

who proceeds from the Father and the Son,
John 14:16–18, 26; 15:26; 20:22

who together with the Father and Son is worshiped and glorified,
Isa 6:3; Matt 28:19; 2 Cor 13:14; Rev 4:8

who spoke by the prophets.
Num 11:29; Mic 3:8; Acts 2:17–18; 2 Pet 1:21

We believe in one holy, catholic, and apostolic Church.
Matt 16:18; 1 Cor 1:2; 10:17; Eph 5:25–28; 1 Tim 3:15; Rev 7:9

We acknowledge one baptism for the forgiveness of sin,
Acts 22:16; Eph 4:4–5; 1 Pet 3:21

And we look for the resurrection of the dead and the life of the age to come.
Isa 11:6–10; Mic 4:1–7; Luke 18:29–30; Rev 21:1–5; 21:22–22:5

Amen.

Memory Verses

Below are suggested memory verses, one for each section of the Creed.

The Father

Rev 4:11 (ESV) — Worthy are you, our Lord and God, to receive glory and honor and power, for you created all things, and by your will they existed and were created.

The Son

John 1:1 (ESV) — In the beginning was the Word, and the Word was with God, and the Word was God.

The Son's Mission

1 Cor 15:3–5 (ESV) — For what I received I passed on to you as of first importance: that Christ died for our sins according to the Scriptures, that he was buried, that he was raised on the third day according to the Scriptures, and that he appeared to Peter, and then to the Twelve.

The Holy Spirit

Rom 8:11 (ESV) — If the Spirit of him who raised Jesus from the dead dwells in you, he who raised Christ Jesus from the dead will also give life to your mortal bodies through his Spirit who dwells in you.

The Church

1 Pet 2:9 (ESV) — But you are a chosen race, a royal priesthood, a holy nation, a people for his own possession, that you may proclaim the excellencies of him who called you out of darkness into his marvelous light.

Our Hope

1 Thess 4:16–17 (ESV) — For the Lord himself will descend from heaven with a cry of command, with the voice of an archangel, and with the sound of the trumpet of God. And the dead in Christ will rise first. Then we who are alive, who are left, will be caught up together with them in the clouds to meet the Lord in the air, and so we will always be with the Lord.

From Before to Beyond Time:
The Plan of God and Human History
Adapted from Suzanne de Dietrich. *God's Unfolding Purpose.*
Philadelphia: Westminster Press, 1976.

I.   Before Time (Eternity Past)

*1 Cor. 2:7 (ESV) – But we impart a secret and hidden wisdom of God,
which God decreed before the ages for our glory (cf. Titus 1:2).*

A. The Eternal Triune God
B. God's Eternal Purpose
C. The Mystery of Iniquity
D. The Principalities and Powers

II. Beginning of Time (Creation and Fall)

Gen. 1:1 (ESV) – In the beginning, God created the heavens and the earth.

A. Creative Word
B. Humanity
C. Fall
D. Reign of Death and First Signs of Grace

III. Unfolding of Time (God's Plan Revealed through Israel)

*Gal. 3:8 (ESV) – And the Scripture, foreseeing that God would justify the
Gentiles by faith, preached the Gospel beforehand to Abraham, saying,
"In you shall all the nations be blessed" (cf. Rom. 9:4-5).*

A. Promise (Patriarchs)
B. Exodus and Covenant at Sinai
C. Promised Land
D. The City, the Temple, and the Throne
    (Prophet, Priest, and King)
E. Exile
F. Remnant

IV. Fullness of Time (Incarnation of the Messiah)

Gal. 4:4-5 (ESV) – But when the fullness of time had come, God sent forth his Son, born of woman, born under the law, to redeem those who were under the law, so that we might receive adoption as sons.

A. The King Comes to His Kingdom
B. The Present Reality of His Reign
C. The Secret of the Kingdom:
   the Already and the Not Yet
D. The Crucified King
E. The Risen Lord

V. The Last Times (The Descent of the Holy Spirit)

Acts 2:16-18 (ESV) – But this is what was uttered through the prophet Joel: "'And in the last days it shall be,' God declares, 'that I will pour out my Spirit on all flesh, and your sons and your daughters shall prophesy, and your young men shall see visions, and your old men shall dream dreams; even on my male servants and female servants in those days I will pour out my Spirit, and they shall prophesy.'"

A. Between the Times: the Church as
   Foretaste of the Kingdom
B. The Church as Agent of the Kingdom
C. The Conflict Between the Kingdoms
   of Darkness and Light

VI. The Fulfillment of Time (The Second Coming)

Matt. 13:40-43 (ESV) – Just as the weeds are gathered and burned with fire, so will it be at the close of the age. The Son of Man will send his angels, and they will gather out of his Kingdom all causes of sin and all lawbreakers, and throw them into the fiery furnace. In that place there will be weeping and gnashing of teeth. Then the righteous will shine like the sun in the Kingdom of their Father. He who has ears, let him hear.

A. The Return of Christ
B. Judgment
C. The Consummation of His Kingdom

VII. Beyond Time (Eternity Future)

1 Cor. 15:24-28 (ESV) – Then comes the end, when he delivers the Kingdom to God the Father after destroying every rule and every authority and power. For he must reign until he has put all his enemies under his feet. The last enemy to be destroyed is death. For "God has put all things in subjection under his feet." But when it says, "all things are put in subjection," it is plain that he is excepted who put all things in subjection under him. When all things are subjected to him, then the Son himself will also be subjected to him who put all things in subjection under him, that God may be all in all.

A. Kingdom Handed Over to God the Father
B. God as All in All

About the Sacred Roots Project

The Sacred Roots Thriving in Ministry Project seeks to equip and empower under-resourced congregational leaders in urban, rural, and incarcerated communities. One avenue for accomplishing this goal is the *Sacred Roots Spiritual Classics*, a series of abridged Christian spiritual classics that equip congregational leaders to engage the wealth of the Great Tradition.

Other *Sacred Roots Spiritual Classics* include:

Praying the Psalms with Augustine and Friends
Edited by Dr. Carmen Joy Imes

Becoming a Community of Disciples:
Guildelines from Abbot Benedict and Bishop Basil
Edited by Rev. Dr. Greg Peters

Spiritual Friendship:
Learning How to Be Friends with God and One Another
Edited by Rev. Dr. Hank Voss

Books Jesus Read: Learning from the Apocrypha
Edited by Dr. Robert F. Lay

Renewal in Christ: Athanasius on the Christian Life
Edited by Rev. Dr. Jeremy Treat

Social Justice and Scripture: The Witness of Las Casas
Edited by Rev. Dr. Robert Chao Romero and
Rev. Marcos Canales

The Senior Editorial Team of the *Sacred Roots Spiritual Classics* includes:

Rev. Dr. Don Davis
Publisher
The Urban Ministry Institute

Rev. Dr. Hank Voss
Executive Editor
Taylor University

Dr. Uche Anizor
Senior Editor
Biola University, Talbot School of Theology

Rev. Dr. Greg Peters
Senior Editor
Biola University, Torrey Honors College

Dr. May Young
Senior Editor
Taylor University

Rev. Ryan Carter
Managing Editor
The Urban Ministry Institute

Isaiah Swain
Managing Editor
Taylor University

The Senior Editorial Team acknowledges and appreciates Dr. Gwenfair Adams (Gordon-Conwell Theological Seminary), Dr. Betsy Barber (Biola University), Rev. Dr.

Nigel Black (Winslow Baptist Church), Dr. Jonathan Calvillo (Boston University School of Divinity), Dr. Laura Edwards (Taylor University), Rev. Nathan Esla (Lutheran Bible Translators), Dr. Nancy Frazier (Dallas Theological Seminary), Dr. Jeff Greenman (Regent College), Dr. Kevin Hector (University of Chicago Divinity School), Rev. Dr. Wil Hernandez (Centerquest), Dr. James Houston (Regent College), Dr. Evan B. Howard (Spirituality Shoppe), Rev. Susie Krehbiel (Missionary, Retired), Rev. Dr. Tim Larsen (Wheaton College), Dr. Stephanie Lowery (Africa International University), Dr. Daniel Owens (Hanoi Bible College), Rev. Dr. Oscar Owens (West Angeles Church of God), Dr. Bob Priest (Taylor University), Rev. Dr. Robert Romero (University of California, Los Angeles), Rev. Dr. Jerry Root (Wheaton College), Dr. Fred Sanders (Biola University), Dr. Glen Scorgie (Bethel University), Dr. Kyle Strobel (Biola University), Dr. Daniel Treier (Wheaton College), and Dr. Kevin Vanhoozer (Trinity Evangelical Divinity School) for their support and encouragement. Illustrations throughout the *Sacred Roots* volumes are done by Naomi Noyes.

The *Sacred Roots Spiritual Classics* are dedicated to all Christian leaders who have loved the poor and have recognized the importance of Christian spiritual classics for nurturing the next generation. We especially recognize these fourteen:

John Wesley (1703–1791)

Rebecca Protten (1718–1780)

Elizabeth Fry (1780–1845)

Phoebe Palmer (1807–1874)

Dora Yu (1873–1931)

A. W. Tozer (1897–1963)

Howard Thurman (1899–1981)

Watchman Nee (1903–1972)

James Houston (1922–)

J. I. Packer (1926–2020)

Tom Oden (1931–2016)

René Padilla (1932–2021)

Dallas Willard (1935–2013)

Bruce Demarest (1935–)

Remember your leaders,
those who spoke to you the word of God.
Consider the outcome of their way of life,
and imitate their faith.

~ Hebrews 13:7

Scripture Index

Made in the USA
Columbia, SC
16 July 2022